ANDERSON'S
Law School Publications

Administrative Law Anthology
Thomas O. Sargentich

Administrative Law: Cases and Materials
Daniel J. Gifford

An Admiralty Law Anthology
Robert M. Jarvis

Alternative Dispute Resolution: Strategies for Law and Business
E. Wendy Trachte-Huber and Stephen K. Huber

The American Constitutional Order: History, Cases, and Philosophy
Douglas W. Kmiec and Stephen B. Presser

American Legal Systems: A Resource and Reference Guide
Toni M. Fine

Analytic Jurisprudence Anthology
Anthony D'Amato

An Antitrust Anthology
Andrew I. Gavil

Appellate Advocacy: Principles and Practice, Third Edition
Ursula Bentele and Eve Cary

Arbitration: Cases and Materials
Stephen K. Huber and E. Wendy Trachte-Huber

Basic Accounting Principles for Lawyers: With Present Value and Expected Value
C. Steven Bradford and Gary A. Ames

A Capital Punishment Anthology (and Electronic Caselaw Appendix)
Victor L. Streib

Cases and Problems in Criminal Law, Third Edition
Myron Moskovitz

The Citation Workbook: How to Beat the Citation Blues, Second Edition
Maria L. Ciampi, Rivka Widerman, and Vicki Lutz

Civil Procedure Anthology
David I. Levine, Donald L. Doernberg, and Melissa L. Nelken

Civil Procedure: Cases, Materials, and Questions, Second Edition
Richard D. Freer and Wendy Collins Perdue

Clinical Anthology: Readings for Live-Client Clinics
Alex J. Hurder, Frank S. Bloch, Susan L. Brooks, and Susan L. Kay

Commercial Transactions Series: Problems and Materials
Louis F. Del Duca, Egon Guttman, Alphonse M. Squillante, Fred H. Miller, Linda Rusch, and Peter Winship
    Vol. 1: Secured Transactions Under the UCC
    Vol. 2: Sales Under the UCC and the CISG
    Vol. 3: Negotiable Instruments Under the UCC and the CIBN

Communications Law: Media, Entertainment, and Regulation
Donald E. Lively, Allen S. Hammond, Blake D. Morant, and Russell L. Weaver

A Conflict-of-Laws Anthology
Gene R. Shreve

Constitutional Conflicts
Derrick A. Bell, Jr.

A Constitutional Law Anthology, Second Edition
Michael J. Glennon, Donald E. Lively, Phoebe A. Haddon, Dorothy E. Roberts, and Russell L. Weaver

Constitutional Law: Cases, History, and Dialogues
Donald E. Lively, Phoebe A. Haddon, Dorothy E. Roberts, and Russell L. Weaver

The Constitutional Law of the European Union
James D. Dinnage and John F. Murphy

The Constitutional Law of the European Union: Documentary Supplement
James D. Dinnage and John F. Murphy

Constitutional Torts
Sheldon H. Nahmod, Michael L. Wells, and Thomas A. Eaton

A Contracts Anthology, Second Edition
Peter Linzer

Contracts: Contemporary Cases, Comments, and Problems
Michael L. Closen, Richard M. Perlmutter, and Jeffrey D. Wittenberg

Contract Law and Practice
Gerald E. Berendt, Michael L. Closen, Doris Estelle Long, Marie A. Monahan, Robert J. Nye, and John H. Scheid

A Copyright Anthology: The Technology Frontier
Richard H. Chused

Corporate Law Anthology
Franklin A. Gevurtz

Corporate and White Collar Crime: An Anthology
Leonard Orland

A Criminal Law Anthology
Arnold H. Loewy

Criminal Law: Cases and Materials
Arnold H. Loewy

A Criminal Procedure Anthology
Silas J. Wasserstrom and Christie L. Snyder

Criminal Procedure: Arrest and Investigation
Arnold H. Loewy and Arthur B. LaFrance

Criminal Procedure: Trial and Sentencing
Arthur B. LaFrance and Arnold H. Loewy

Economic Regulation: Cases and Materials
Richard J. Pierce, Jr.

Elements of Law
Eva H. Hanks, Michael E. Herz, and Steven S. Nemerson

Ending It: Dispute Resolution in America
　Descriptions, Examples, Cases and Questions
Susan M. Leeson and Bryan M. Johnston

An Environmental Law Anthology
Robert L. Fischman, Maxine I. Lipeles, and Mark S. Squillace

Environmental Law Series
Jackson B. Battle, Robert L. Fischman, Maxine I. Lipeles, and Mark S. Squillace
    Vol. 1: Environmental Decisionmaking: NEPA and the Endangered Species Act,
        Second Edition
    Vol. 2: Water Pollution, Third Edition
    Vol. 3: Air Pollution, Third Edition
    Vol. 4: Hazardous Waste, Third Edition

Environmental Protection and Justice
   Readings and Commentary on Environmental Law and Practice
Kenneth A. Manaster

European Union Law Anthology
Karen V. Kole and Anthony D'Amato

An Evidence Anthology
Edward J. Imwinkelried and Glen Weissenberger

Federal Antitrust Law: Cases and Materials
Daniel J. Gifford and Leo J. Raskind

Federal Income Tax Anthology
Paul L. Caron, Karen C. Burke, and Grayson M.P. McCouch

Federal Rules of Civil Procedure, 1998-99 Edition
Publisher's Staff

Federal Rules of Evidence Handbook, 1998-99 Edition
Publisher's Staff

Federal Rules of Evidence: Rules, Legislative History, Commentary and Authority
   1998-99 Edition
Glen Weissenberger

Federal Wealth Transfer Tax Anthology
Paul L. Caron, Grayson M.P. McCouch, Karen C. Burke

First Amendment Anthology
Donald E. Lively, Dorothy E. Roberts, and Russell L. Weaver

The History, Philosophy, and Structure of the American Constitution
Douglas W. Kmiec and Stephen B. Presser

Individual Rights and the American Constitution
Douglas W. Kmiec and Stephen B. Presser

International Environmental Law Anthology
Anthony D'Amato and Kirsten Engel

International Human Rights: Law, Policy, and Process, Second Edition
Frank C. Newman and David Weissbrodt

Selected International Human Rights Instruments and
   Bibliography For Research on International Human Rights Law, Second Edition
Frank C. Newman and David Weissbrodt

International Intellectual Property Anthology
Anthony D'Amato and Doris Estelle Long

International Law Anthology
Anthony D'Amato

International Law Coursebook
Anthony D'Amato

Introduction to the Study of Law: Cases and Materials
John Makdisi

Judicial Externships: The Clinic Inside the Courthouse
Rebecca A. Cochran

A Land Use Anthology
Jon W. Bruce

Law and Economics Anthology
Kenneth G. Dau-Schmidt and Thomas S. Ulen

The Law of Disability Discrimination, Second Edition
Ruth Colker and Bonnie P. Tucker

ADA Handbook: Statutes, Regulations and Related Materials
Publisher's Staff

Lawyers and Fundamental Moral Responsibility
Daniel R. Coquillette

Mediation and Negotiation: Reaching Agreement in Law and Business
E. Wendy Trachte-Huber and Stephen K. Huber

Microeconomic Predicates to Law and Economics
Mark Seidenfeld

Natural Resources: Cases and Materials
Barlow Burke

Patients, Psychiatrists and Lawyers: Law and the Mental Health System, Second Edition
Raymond L. Spring, Roy B. Lacoursiere, and Glen Weissenberger

Preventive Law: Materials on a Non Adversarial Legal Process
Robert M. Hardaway

Principles of Evidence, Third Edition
Irving Younger, Michael Goldsmith, and David A. Sonenshein

Problems and Simulations in Evidence, Second Edition
Thomas F. Guernsey

A Products Liability Anthology
Anita Bernstein

Professional Responsibility Anthology
Thomas B. Metzloff

A Property Anthology, Second Edition
Richard H. Chused

Public Choice and Public Law: Readings and Commentary
Maxwell L. Stearns

Readings in Criminal Law
Russell L. Weaver, John M. Burkoff, Catherine Hancock, Alan Reed, and Peter J. Seago

Science in Evidence
D.H. Kaye

A Section 1983 Civil Rights Anthology
Sheldon H. Nahmod

Sports Law: Cases and Materials, Third Edition
Ray L. Yasser, James R. McCurdy, and C. Peter Goplerud

A Torts Anthology
Lawrence C. Levine, Julie A. Davies, and Edward J. Kionka

Trial Practice
Lawrence A. Dubin and Thomas F. Guernsey

Unincorporated Business Entities
Larry E. Ribstein

FORTHCOMING PUBLICATIONS

Cases and Materials on the Law Governing Lawyers
James E. Moliterno

Corporations Law: Cases and Materials
William A. Gregory and Thomas R. Hurst

Environmental Decisionmaking: NEPA, and the Endangered Species Act, Third Edition
Jackson B. Battle, Robert L. Fischman, and Mark S. Squillace

International Civil Procedure Anthology
David S. Clark and Anthony D'Amato

International Taxation: Cases, Materials, and Problems
Philip F. Postlewaite

Judicial Externships: The Clinic Inside the Courthouse, Second Edition
Rebecca A. Cochran

Resolution of Private International Disputes
David D. Caron

A Torts Anthology, Second Edition
Lawrence C. Levine, Julie Anne Davies, Edward J. Kionka

Microeconomic Predicates to Law and Economics

MICROECONOMIC PREDICATES TO LAW AND ECONOMICS

MARK SEIDENFELD

PROFESSOR OF LAW
THE FLORIDA STATE UNIVERSITY COLLEGE OF LAW

ANDERSON PUBLISHING CO.
CINCINNATI, OHIO

MICROECONOMIC PREDICATES TO LAW AND ECONOMICS
MARK SEIDENFELD

©1996 by Anderson Publishing Co.

Second Printing – September, 1998

2035 Reading Road / Cincinnati, Ohio 45202
800-582-7295 / e-mail andpubco@aol.com / Fax 513-562-5430
World Wide Web http://www.andersonpublishing.com

All rights reserved. No part of this book may be reproduced in any form or by any electronic or mechanical means including information storage and retrieval systems without permission in writing from the publisher.

ISBN: 0-87084-804-6

To my father, who instilled in me an appreciation of abstract thought, and to the memory of my mother, who taught me that abstract thought alone never accomplished anything.

Table of Contents

Preface xvii
Introduction 1
    Suggested Additional Reading 3

Chapter 1 Consumer Choice and Demand 5

  A. Consumer Preferences and a Theory of Constrained Choice 5
      1. The rational consumer and utility 5
      2. Consumer indifference curves 6
      3. Constrained consumer choice and budget lines 7
      4. The consumer's optimal choice—maximization of utility 8
      5. The assumption of exogenous preferences 10
  B. Consumer Responses to Price Changes and the Concept of Market Demand 10
      1. Individual consumption as a function of price 10
      2. Income and substitution effects of price changes 12
      3. Market demand 13
      4. Elasticity of demand 14
      5. Consumer surplus 16
      6. Using indifference curves and budget lines to answer economic
         questions—an example 17
    Suggested Additional Reading 19

Chapter 2 Producer Decisions—Cost, Revenue and Profit Maximization 21

  A. Producers' Cost Functions 21
      1. Opportunity cost 21
      2. Efficient use of resources and the total cost function 22
      3. Marginal cost and average cost, and their relationship to total cost .. 24
      4. Fixed costs and variable costs 28
  B. Producers' Decisions: Profit Maximization and the Level of Production ... 28
      1. The Meaning of economic profit 28
      2. Choosing the level of production that maximizes profit: the relationship of
         marginal revenue and marginal cost to profit maximization 29
      3. Deciding whether to enter into a business: the relationship between price,
         average cost and economic profit 29
      4. Choosing the profit maximizing level of production of shoes given a cost
         function—an example 31
    Suggested Additional Reading 34

Chapter 3 Market Dynamics and Equilibrium ... 35

A. Purely Competitive Markets ... 35
   1. Competitive markets in the short run ... 36
   2. Competitive markets in the long run ... 37
B. Monopoly Markets ... 39
   1. A comparison of social wealth under monopoly and competition ... 40
   2. Price discriminating monopolies and social wealth ... 42
C. Government Intervention into Markets ... 44
   Suggested Additional Reading ... 48

Chapter 4 Efficiency & Social Welfare ... 49

A. The Pareto Criterion for Efficiency ... 49
   1. Distributional Efficiency and the Edgeworth Box ... 49
   2. Productive efficiency ... 51
   3. Allocative efficiency ... 52
   4. Problems with the Pareto criteria for efficiency ... 54
B. The Kaldor-Hicks Criteria for Efficiency and Wealth Maximization ... 54
C. Other Social Welfare Functions and the Theory of Public Choice ... 56
   1. Equality as a social value and John Rawls maximin principle ... 56
   2. Legislative determination of social welfare and public choice theory ... 57
   Suggested Additional Reading ... 60

Chapter 5 Market Imperfections ... 61

A. Natural Monopolies ... 61
B. Externalities ... 63
   1. External costs ... 63
   2. External benefits ... 65
C. Imperfect Information ... 66
D. Transaction Costs ... 67
   Suggested Additional Reading ... 68

Chapter 6 Uncertainty, Risk and Insurance ... 69

A. Probability Distributions of Outcomes and Risk ... 69
   1. Probability distributions of outcomes ... 69
   2. Expected value and risk ... 69
B. Expected Utility ... 70
C. Insurance ... 73

Chapter 6–*Continued*
    1. The moral hazard problem 74
    2. The adverse selection problem 74
    3. Example: Joe's drinking problem, the benefits of insurance, and the need for "deductibles" 75
    Suggested Additional Reading 77

Chapter 7 Choices over Time—Decisions about Lending and Investing 79
A. The Time Value of Money 79
    1. The interest rate for borrowing and lending 79
    2. The present value of future payouts 81
    3. Investment to produce goods in the future 81
B. Risk and Return 83
    Suggested Additional Reading 84

Chapter 8 Strategic Behavior and Game Theory 85
A. Normal Form Games 85
B. Nash Equilibrium 86
C. Extensive Form Games 87
    Suggested Additional Reading 90

Chapter 9 Coase's Theorem—Efficient Allocation of Legal Entitlements 91
    Suggested Additional Reading 94

Index 95

Preface

This book stems from materials I prepared for students in my Law and Economics Course at Florida State University. Because I do not require that students have any economics background as a prerequisite for this course, I spend the first several weeks of the course introducing the economics concepts that I use in evaluating various legal doctrines. Unfortunately, I did not find any Law and Economics texts that provided what I considered to be a sufficient overview of economics.

Some Law and Economics texts seem purposely to avoid analytic rigor in discussing underlying economic principles. Sensitive to law students aversion to equations and graphs, I began teaching the course using one of these texts. I found, however, that students frequently responded to the lack of analytic rigor by failing to differentiate fuzzy from precise thinking, for example by reasoning from examples that did not generalize to more universal propositions. Other texts were more rigorous in their treatment of economics, but left many fundamental concepts unexplained until they were needed for a particular legal analysis. When I used one of these texts, I found that the complexity of the legal issue whose analysis prompted introduction of the novel economic concepts confused the students. This reinforced my intuition that students best learn how to apply economics to law if they have already been introduced to the economic concepts in an orderly and coherent manner.

Thus, perhaps by trial and error, I was led to assign a separate Microeconomics text in addition to the primary Law and Economics text I used. I found that Microeconomics texts generally included most of the information that I needed to present to the students. Unfortunately, these texts included much more than the students needed to know, and picking and choosing my way through the text often disrupted the very coherence of presentation that prompted me to assign a supplementary text in the first place. In addition, the emphases of these texts tended to downplay many issues I consider important, including the significance and reality of the assumptions underlying economic models, and the value choices underlying the economic measure of goodness—efficiency. Finally, many students complained about the expense of a text that they used only for the first few weeks of the course.

In the summer of 1995, I wrote and distributed to my students in Law and Economics a set of notes on "Microeconomic Predicates to Law and Economics" as a supplement to the primary Law and Economic text that I used. The students enjoyed the straightforward approach of the notes, and their understanding of how economics applied to legal reasoning seemed to improve. This book is an expanded version of those notes, and is intended primarily as a supplement to existing Law and Economics texts. The chapters on efficiency, intertemporal choice and Coase's theorem, however, might also provide short but rigorous backgrounds to economic concepts used in traditional first year courses, an introductory course on philosophical approaches to law, and a course on corporate finance.

In this book, I present the microeconomic fundamentals necessary to evaluate legal doctrines in a rigorous manner without introducing what many law students consider to be complex mathematics such as calculus or even sophisticated analytic geometry. Where mathematical tools are helpful, such as in explaining the notions of budget constraints and marginality, I develop the necessary mathematical concepts in the book. I do rely heavily on graphical analyses to develop economic concepts. Nonetheless, I have found that students with economics backgrounds or strong analytic abilities can work their way through the book without too much difficulty. Students with neither an economics nor analytic background can also work their way through the book if they make the effort and are given some support by review of the material in the classroom and assignments of homework exercises that reinforce the materials in the text.

The book emphasizes those aspects of microeconomic theory that I have found most important to the evaluation of economic models of the impact of legal rules. Most of the illustrations of economic concepts draw on examples which should be familiar and of interest to law students. I have found that this helps maintain law students' interest in the abstract economics until we finally apply the concepts in the book in a more concrete setting. Overall, I hope that, like the notes from which this primer on microeconomics stems, this book will ease students' transition into thinking economically about issues of law.

Introduction

Law and Economics focuses on using economic theory to help apply, understand and evaluate law. Economics enters into law in at least three ways. First, legal outcomes in particular cases depend on the facts of those cases. Economics can help one make factual determinations. For a simple example of how economics can facilitate such fact-finding one need look no further than a tort case in which a worker has been disabled. If the worker prevails on her claim, she is entitled to receive compensation for the harm caused by the tortious act. But what is the value to her of the wages that she loses because of the disability? Economics indicates how to reduce a future income stream to a single present value.

Second, some laws regulate conduct in explicit economic terms. In order to understand these laws, one must understand the economic concepts on which they rely. For example, antitrust law prohibits monopolization. Economics gives a definition of monopoly and explains why monopolies generally are not good for society. These economic concepts, in turn, give meaning to the law and help courts and regulators fashion legal doctrines to implement the law effectively.

Third, economics provides some measure of what is "good." Thus, lawyers can use economics to critique legal doctrines. In addition, borrowing the economic notion of "goodness" allows a litigator to generate persuasive arguments about whether legal rules should be changed or the bounds of their application limited. An example, which we will consider in detail later in the course, is whether to allow a tort action against a manufacturer for producing a product that causes harm even if the product is nonetheless valuable and the manufacturer has taken sufficient care in its production to minimize such harm. In other words, should society prefer strict liability to negligence for harm caused by products? Although economics will rarely provide "the right answer" to such questions about the strictures of legal rules, it will help illuminate the impact of adopting one rule versus the other, and will give some guidance about which is likely to make society better off as a whole.

The branch of economics which most directly bears on legal issues is microeconomics. Microeconomics is the study of how a decision-making unit, such as an individual, a firm, a governmental body, or even a judge, reacts to changes in economic circumstances, such as prices, costs, income and even legal rules.[1] As such, we should not be surprised that microeconomics has much to say about law. Microeconomics addresses how decision-makers will behave in response to circumstances and, after all, law is the means by which the government constrains and influences behavior.

Microeconomics posits a theory of human behavior, which it calls economic rationality, and makes simplifying assumptions about the attributes of the market or of the transaction of interest. It uses this theory and its simplified description of the relevant economic world to create analytically rigorous models that predict the outcome that would occur in this simplified world. By comparing the economic model to the real world, microeconomics can often predict

---

[1] The other major branch of economics, macroeconomics, deals instead with the relationships and movements of aggregate economic measures such as gross national product, unemployment rates, inflation rates and money supplies.

CONCEPT OF EFFICIENCY

approximate real world outcomes. Perhaps of greater significance for actors on the legal stage, microeconomic models can give insights into the reasons that these results occur, allowing lawmakers to tailor legal rules so that these rules are more likely to induce the behavior that society seeks. This is the positive or descriptive aspect of microeconomics.

In addition to providing descriptions and explanations of economic outcomes, microeconomics also has a normative aspect. It defines a measure of economic "goodness," which it calls efficiency. By predicting how resources will be allocated under various legal rules and comparing these predictions to its measures of efficiency, microeconomics provides a means to evaluate whether particular legal outcomes are preferable to others.

Unlike in the straight study of economics, using the concept of efficiency in legal analysis is controversial. Many economists see their role as describing economic outcomes or evaluating which of several outcomes is preferable, **accepting as given individuals' own assessment of what they like and the economic definition of efficiency**. Many economists would not include questioning the definition of efficiency within the scope of their tasks. Lawyers, however, concern themselves with such grand notions as justice and fairness. Frequently laws are intended to influence an individual's fundamental values and personal ethics. Thus, the study of microeconomics for lawyers stresses different aspects of the subject. In addition to creating economic models to predict and evaluate outcomes, we will spend a great deal of time questioning the assumptions underlying those models. We will ask whether those assumptions are unrealistic in a way that influences the models' predicted outcomes. Finally, we will ask whether the assumptions, even if realistic, bias the analysis towards outcomes that society would consider improper or unjust.

At this juncture, an example of an economic model that bears on a legal question will help illuminate the possible interplay between economics and law, as well as set limits on that interplay. Consider the question of whether the government should raise the minimum wage. Standard economic models analyze such a raise as an increase in the cost of labor to producers. They predict that an increase in the minimum wage will result in fewer low wage jobs. The decrease in such jobs may be so great that it is unclear whether low wage earners as a class will benefit: some will benefit as a result of the increased wage, but others will be hurt because they will be out of work due to the decease in jobs.

Thus far, the model has been merely descriptive. The normative aspect of economics, however, counsels that increasing the minimum wage will be inefficient. There will be some workers out of a job who would be willing to work for less than the new minimum wage, and some employers who do not offer jobs at the new wage who would be willing to do so at a lower wage. These workers and employers would both be better off if the government let them bargain for a wage below the increased minimum. Raising the wage will increase the number of individuals who would be prohibited from reaching such a bargain.

Nonetheless, society might prefer the increased minimum wage despite its inefficiency for several reasons. First, the descriptive economic model might be inaccurate: there is some data suggesting that workers facing decreases in pay do not behave as economically rational actors.[2] Because feelings of self worth are often tied to the wage one receives, employees might derive

---

[2] *See* Lester Thurow, GENERATING INEQUALITIES 77 (1975).

a value from a high wage independent of the buying power of the money itself. In such a case, a worker might choose to refuse to work at a lower wage than she believes she deserves, even if she cannot garner her just wage anywhere in the job market. Ultimately, this choice might affect how an employer values the work of his employees. In other words, raising the minimum wage might affect the value that workers place on their work that in turn will affect their willingness to work for a lower wage and an employer's willingness to offer them a higher wage.

Second, even if the model is descriptively accurate, society may choose not to act efficiently. Cultural norms might lead citizens to prefer a minimum wage that pays "an honest wage for an honest day's work." In other words, people might value notions of fairness above efficiency so that as a society they would gladly pay the price of a just, if inefficient, minimum wage.

This example illustrates the potential power of economic models and their potential limitations. Armed with our understanding of economic models, and keeping in mind caveats about use of such models, it is time to begin our foray into the world of microeconomics.

Suggested Additional Reading

Jon Elster, SOLOMONIC JUDGEMENTS: STUDIES IN THE LIMITATIONS OF RATIONALITY 1-35 (1989).

Milton Friedman, *The Methodology of Positive Economics*, in Milton Friedman, ESSAYS IN POSITIVE ECONOMICS 3-43 (1953).

Arthur E. Leff, *Economic Analysis of Law: Some Realism About Nominalism*, 60 VA. L. REV. 451 (1974).

A.K. Klevorick, *Law and Economics: An Economist's View*, 65 AM. ECON. REV. 237, 237-43 (1975).

Werner Z. Hirsch, LAW AND ECONOMICS: AN INTRODUCTORY ANALYSIS 2-11 (2d ed. 1988).

Frank H. Knight, THE ECONOMIC ORGANIZATION 3-31 (1951).

Cento G. Veljanovski, *The New Law-and-Economics: A Research Review*, reprinted in READINGS IN THE ECONOMICS OF LAW AND REGULATION 12-25 (A. I. Ogus & C.G. Veljanovski, eds. 1984).

1
Consumer Choice and Demand

The primary decision-makers in economic markets are consumers and producers. We begin our study of economics by modeling how consumers make economic decisions. We do so for several reasons. First, laws often restrict consumer choices or raise prices to consumers. We would like to know how consumers will react to such restrictions or price increases. For example, we might like to know what consumers will do if states increase their cigarette taxes. Will smokers smoke less or will they instead give up some other product on which they spend money in order to pay the higher price? To what extent might smokers attempt to avoid the tax by buying bootleg cigarettes? The study of consumer choices will provide insights into answering such questions. In particular, it will demonstrate how consumer choices lead to demand functions for a product, which are crucial to understanding how the market for the product functions.

Second, the theory of consumer choices will also illuminate how individuals might interact outside of a market transaction. This is very significant for legal analysis because law often applies to such individual dealing. In economics, the model we will use for such non-market transactions is one of two consumers bartering two goods, but the insights generalize to other contexts. For example, such a bartering model will have much to say about any contract between individuals, such as one might negotiate when buying a used car from a prior owner.

A. Consumer Preferences and a Theory of Constrained Choice

1. The rational consumer and utility

To begin, economists posit a simplified model of how consumers make choices. The economist assumes that the consumer faces choices about what "market-basket" of goods to buy. A market-basket is merely a set of specific quantities of available goods. Economists assume that consumers compare market-baskets and choose between them according to the following assumptions:

(i) For any two market-baskets, A and B, either the consumer prefers A to B, prefers B to A, or is indifferent between A and B. Consumers act consistently over the time frame in which our analysis occurs. In other words, if the consumer prefers A to B now, she will also prefer A to B later.

(ii) If a consumer prefers market-basket A to B, and market-basket B to C, then she will prefer A to C.

(iii) Goods are good things, so all else being equal, a consumer wants more of them. Thus if market-basket A differs from market-basket B only because A has less of some good than B, the consumer will prefer B to A.

(iv) A consumer derives diminishing marginal utility from goods. The more a consumer has of a good, the less she values each unit of that good relative to other goods.

(v) The consumer acts to obtain the market-basket that she prefers most out of all those that she can possibly obtain.

These assumptions seem logical, and economists therefore refer to a consumer who follows them as a "rational" consumer. But, in legal analysis there are situations in which these assumptions do not hold true. We must always remember to question whether we believe that these assumptions are accurate before accepting the teaching of any economic model.

To ease the comprehension of these assumptions, we can assign numbers to market-baskets, ordering them by the consumer's preference. If we call these numbers "utility' then all of our assumptions come down to assertions that consumers place more utility on the first few units of a good than on later units, and rational consumers maximize utility. We must be careful, however, not to oversimplify; therefore we must remember that utility is merely a means of ordering preferences for a particular individual. There is no absolute meaning to the numbers we assign as utility. For example, we could take any such assignment for an individual and multiply the numbers by ten, and the new numbers would work just as well as the original numbers. Most significantly, this means that utility is only a means of comparing choices for one individual; it cannot be used to compare the preferences of one consumer with those of another.

2. *Consumer indifference curves*

Economists like to have graphs to represent their theories, and the theory of consumer choice is no exception. We cannot graph all the goods available to a consumer on a two-dimensional page but luckily we can graph an economic universe consisting of only two goods without losing any of the ideas underlying the theory of consumer choice. So, without loss of generality, let's consider the choices facing a consumer (call him Al) who can purchase either food or clothing.

We start by graphing lines that connect market-baskets between which Al is indifferent. These curves are called Al's indifference curves and are graphed in Figure 1. Because of our assumptions, these curves will be convex to the origin, and non-intersecting, and Al will prefer points on curves farther from the origin to those on curves closer to the origin. Note from the curves in Figure 1 that Al is indifferent between 6 outfits of clothing and 1 meal of food, 4 outfits and 2 meals, 3 outfits and 3 meals, and 2 outfits and 5 meals. We have only graphed representative indifference curves. From the assumption that a consumer can order any two market-baskets, it follows that every market-basket is on some indifference curve; there is no market-basket that Al does not either prefer more, less or the same as other market-baskets. In other words, although we have shown only three indifference curves, in fact indifference curves that are not shown fill up the entire area of the graph.

Consider now the point on a curve where the slope of the curve is -2. (Recall that the slope of a straight line is $\Delta y/\Delta x$. The slope of a curve at a point is the slope of the tangent to the curve at that point). This point is represented by **X** on the graph. At this point, Al would be indifferent between trading two units of clothing for one of food. We can see this graphically by noting that for small changes in quantities of food and clothing, if Al gives up twice as many units of clothing as he adds units of food, he remains on the same indifference curve. We say that his "marginal rate of substitution" of clothing for food at this point is 2.

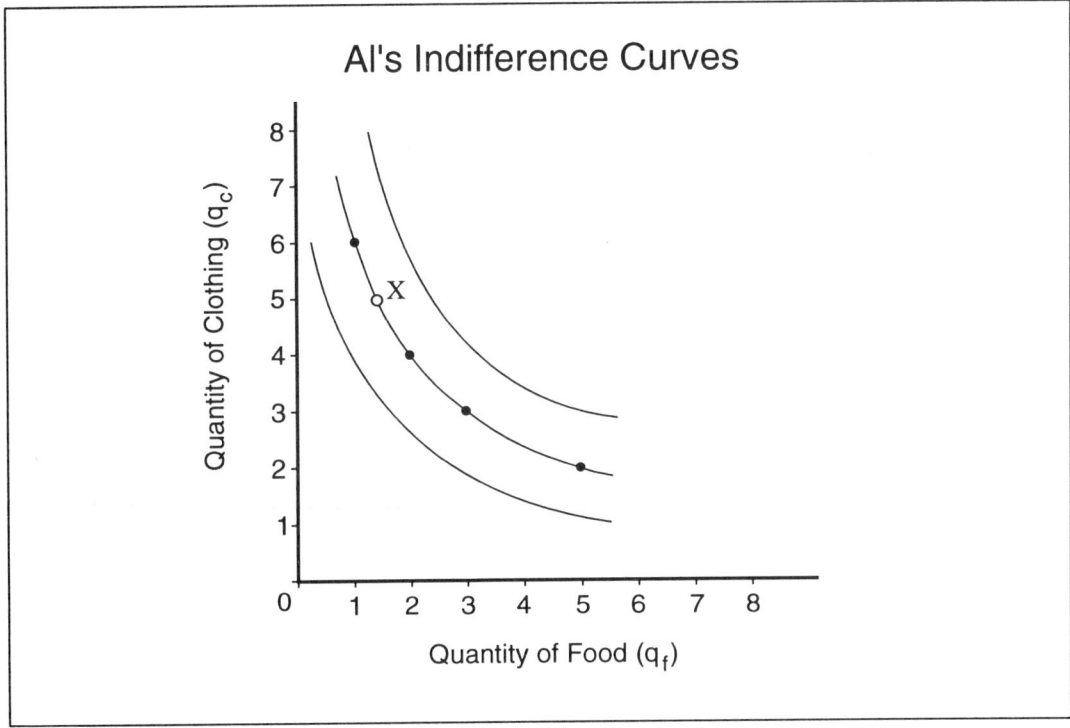

Figure 1

3. *Constrained consumer choice and budget lines*

Once we know Al's preferences, we want to know which market-basket he will purchase. To study this, however, we have to put a constraint on what Al can buy. (Otherwise, given our definition of utility, he would purchase an infinite quantity of food and clothing.) Not surprisingly, the constraint on how much Al can purchase is his income or wealth (which we consider synonymous for purposes of the theory of consumer choice). Suppose that Al's income (I) is $80, the price of food ($p_f$) is $20 per meal, and the price of clothing (p_c) is $10 per outfit. How much food and clothing will Al buy?

We can answer this question by using our graph of Al's indifference curves. To do so, however, we must first introduce a concept known as the budget line. The budget line represents all the market-baskets that the consumer, Al, can purchase. To buy q_f units of food, Al will have to spend $q_f \cdot p_f$. Similarly, to buy q_c units of clothing, he will have to spend $q_c \cdot p_c$. Because Al can buy only food and clothing, his income must equal the sum of the amount he spends on food and the amount he spends on clothing. Thus, for any income level, the market-baskets that Al can afford are given by the following equation:

$$I = q_f \cdot p_f + q_c \cdot p_c$$

Hence, this is the equation for Al's budget line for income I. The budget line is aptly named,

8 MICROECONOMIC PREDICATES TO LAW AND ECONOMICS

as the equation above describes a straight line. One can see this by solving for the variable along the vertical axis, giving $q_c = -(p_f/p_c) \cdot q_f + I/p_c$.[3] It has a negative slope of p_f/p_c, the ratio of the prices of the two goods. It has a vertical intercept of I/p_c, which represents the number of units of clothing that Al could buy if he spent no money on food. Similarly, it has a horizontal intercept of I/p_{fg}, which represents the number of units of food Al could buy if he spent no money on clothing.

For a given set of prices, we could graph a series of budget lines each representing the market-baskets that the consumer could afford at a particular income level. A graph of Al's budget lines for incomes of $40, $60 and $80, given a price of food of $20 per meal and a price of clothing of $10 per outfit, is shown in Figure 2.

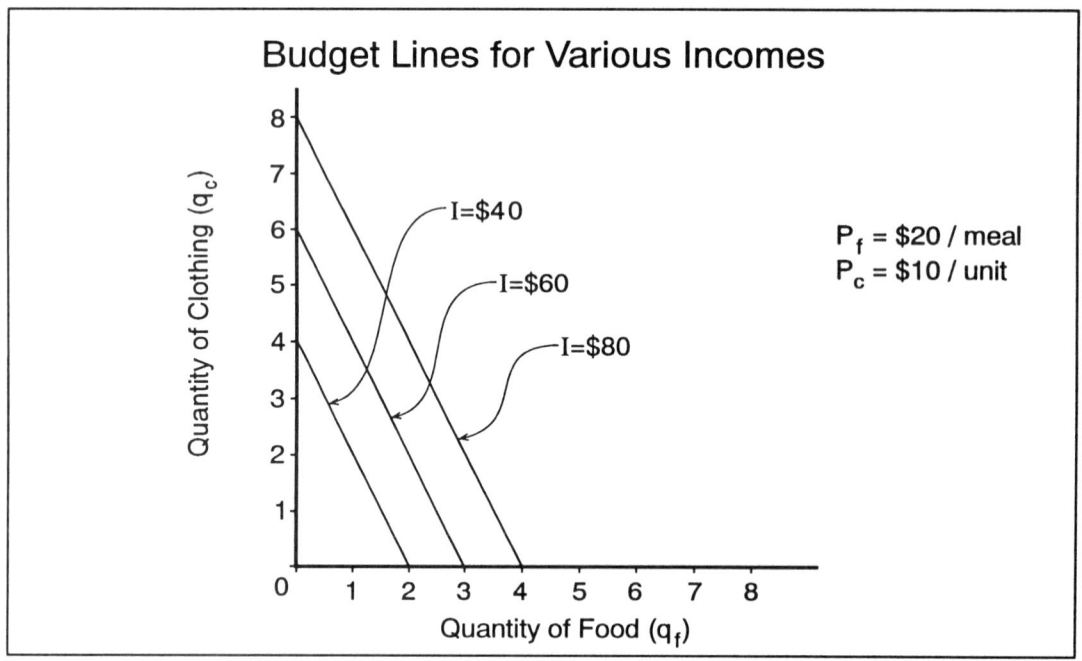

Figure 2

4. *The consumer's optimal choice—maximization of utility*

To determine how much food and clothing Al would buy, given an income of $80, we graph the budget line for this income on the same graph as Al's indifference curves. This is shown in Figure 3. Because the budget line represents the bound of the market-baskets that Al can afford, we follow this budget line until we reach the highest indifference curve with which it

---

[3] Some of you might recall that the equation for a straight line is $Y = mX + b$, where Y is the variable along the vertical axis, X the variable along the horizontal axis, m the slope of the line and b the intercept of the Y axis. If you do not recall this, you can easily verify it by noting that every increase of one unit of X, results in an increase in mX units of Y. Hence the slope of this curve at every point ($\Delta Y/\Delta X$) is $mX/X = m$. Since the slope does not change as one moves along the curve, the curve is a straight line. The Y intercept is the value of the curve at $X=0$, which is b. If you are not familiar with this equation, you might want to take some time graphing the curves corresponding to various values of m and b, until you are feel comfortable that the curves are straight lines as described above.

intersects. The point at which the budget line intersects the highest indifference curve it touches represents the market-basket Al will buy. Al cannot reach any market-basket that he prefers more than that represented by this point.

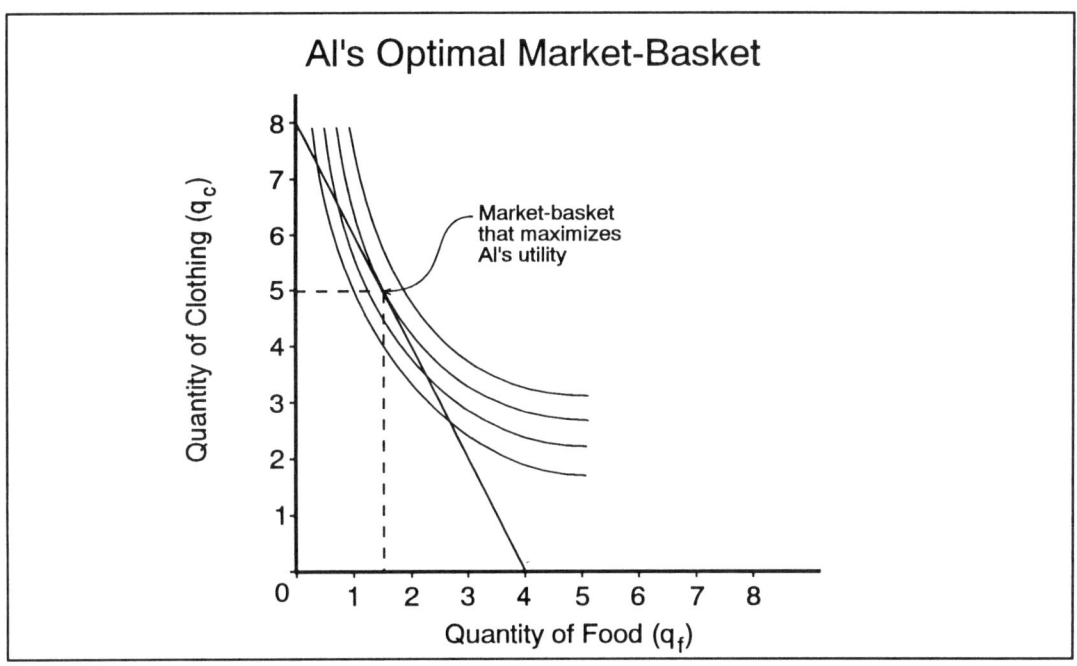

Figure 3

Al's optimal market-basket (the one that maximizes his utility) cannot fall at any point where his budget line crosses an indifference curve. At such a point Al can always increase his utility by changing the quantity of goods he buys to move up and to the right of the indifference curve for that point. Thus, the point representing the market-basket that maximizes Al's utility, subject to his budget constraint, usually will fall where the budget line is tangent to an indifference curve, as is shown in Figure 3.[4]

The graph in Figure 3 illustrates an interesting point about markets in which the price of goods is the same for every consumer. Because the consumer purchases the market-basket represented by the point where the budget line is tangent to her indifference curve, the slope of the budget line is the marginal rate of substitution for the consumer. But the slope of the budget line is the ratio of the prices of the goods we graphed. Hence, in a market where all consumers face the same prices, every consumer has the same marginal rate of substitution of any good for any other good. For the prices we have assumed exist in the market, every consumer will be willing to trade two outfits of clothing for one meal, as each of these is worth $20. In other words, price works like a mechanism to allocate goods in such a way that consumers cannot

---

[4] Technically Al's optimal market-basket may fall on one of the axes; when it does, the market-basket is known as a corner solution. Corner solutions are not the norm for basic goods because they represent a point at which the consumer purchases zero units of one of the goods.

make themselves better off by swapping goods with each other.

5. *The assumption of exogenous preferences*

Before proceeding any further with our study of consumer choice, it is necessary to point out that we have implicitly added an assumption about consumer preferences when we combined Al's budget line and his indifference curves. We assumed that Al's preferences about goods do not change with his income. This is part of a larger assumption that microeconomists make about consumer preferences; they assume such preferences are **exogenous** to the economic system. To say that preferences are exogenous means that they are not dependent on economic variables such as the price of goods or a consumer's income, or how much of the goods others purchase.

Of course this does not mean that the relative quantities of goods that a consumer purchases will not vary as prices and income vary. But, such variations occur because of the changes in the budget line of the consumer overlaid on a stable set of indifference curves. The assumption of exogenous preferences just means that the indifference curves themselves do not change as the economic variables change.

Nonetheless, many law and economics scholars consider the assumption of exogenous preferences to be controversial. Some preferences clearly change with economic outcomes. When a person attends college, that is the purchase of a good: education. But the very act of consuming the good tends to alter that person's values. As the student learns about different options and lifestyles, develops a new set of friends, etc., she is almost certain to desire different goods and services. Thus, before you apply the theory of consumer choice in any particular context, you must make sure that the context is not likely to be one for which the economic variables or economic choices of the consumer significantly change the values and preferences of the consumer.[5]

B. Consumer Responses to Price Changes and the Concept of Market Demand

1. *Individual consumption as a function of price*

We have now developed the rudiments of a theory for determining how consumers choose between various goods in the marketplace. To fully understand consumer choice, however, we

---

[5] Of course, such outputs and choices always have some effect on individuals' values and preferences. These effects, however, are not damning to economic theory as long as the effects are small enough that they do not negate the insights provided by the theory. Thus, the assumption of exogenous consumer preferences is not problematic unless a variable in the economic model is one that is likely to cause relatively significant changes in consumer preferences. It was for this reason that we were skeptical about the microeconomic model of the minimum wage increase in the introduction: we suspected that the value workers place on their labor would change with the prevailing level of wages. For this reason, one might also look with suspicion on a neo-classical economic model aimed at predicting the consumption of a good that advertises itself as the most expensive one available because part of the value of the good comes from the prestige of being able to pay such a high price. But, for modeling production and consumption of most goods, microeconomic models are not greatly plagued by problems of endogenous preferences.

will need to understand how consumers respond to changes in the prices of goods. To investigate this question, we must assume that only the price of one good changes. We assume that the price of all other goods stays the same. In addition, we assume that consumers' incomes stay the same. With these assumptions, we can investigate how price changes affect budget lines. (At this point we are interested in the consumption of a single good relative to all other goods. Hence, we will not use graphs of two particular goods, but rather we will graph on the horizontal axis the quantity of the good in which we are interested, and on the vertical axis the money spent on all other goods. This doesn't affect the ideas presented in the graphs and is convenient because the vertical intercept of each income curve then corresponds to the income for the curve.)

As the price of the good increases, the amount of the good the consumer can buy (the x-intercept) decreases. If the consumer does not purchase any of the good whose price increases, she is unaffected by the price increase. In other words, the value of the y-intercept remains unchanged. Knowing this we can graph various budget lines corresponding to various prices of the good in which we are interested. Figure 4 depicts this graph.

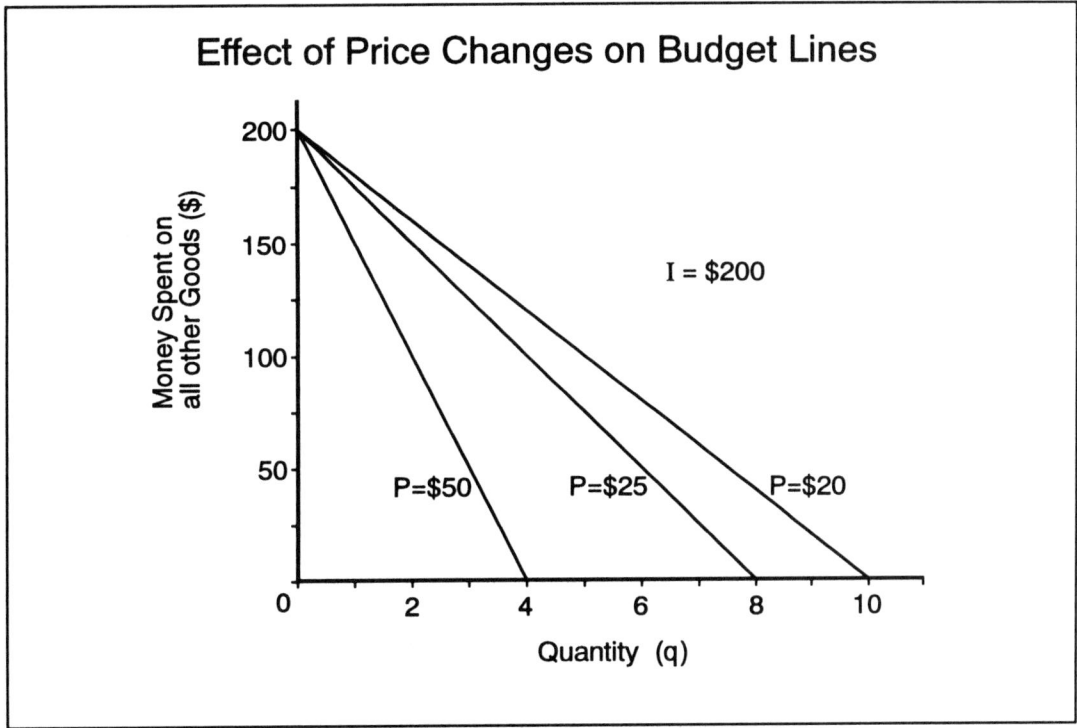

Figure 4

To see how our consumer Al responds to a price change, we can superimpose the budget lines corresponding to the original price and the new price of the good on his indifference curves. By doing this, we can read off the amount of the good Al purchases under each price and see the effect of the price change on his purchase of the good. This is shown in Figure 5.

12 MICROECONOMIC PREDICATES TO LAW AND ECONOMICS

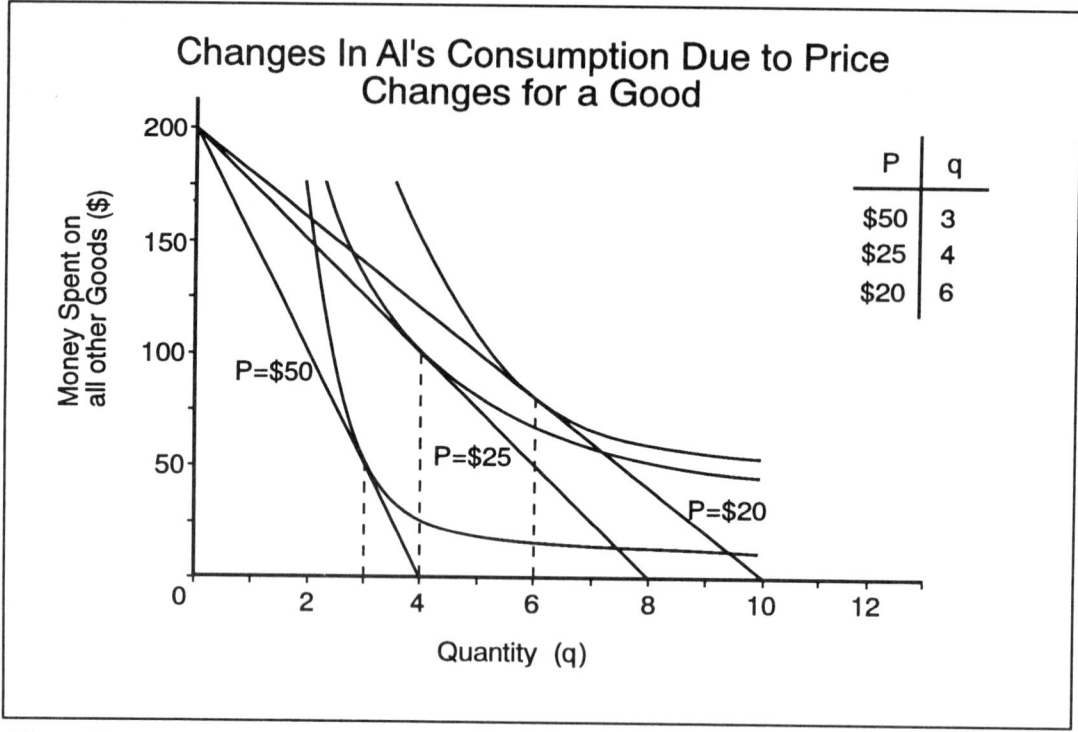

Figure 5

2. *Income and substitution effects of price changes*

As is true given the curves in this graph, as the price of a good increases, the amount the consumer buys of the good generally decreases.[6] But there are two reasons why the amount of the good consumed changes. The first is that the good becomes more expensive relative to other goods. Hence, consumers tend to look for substitutes for the good. If salmon becomes expensive, then perhaps cod will have to do. This tendency is known as the substitution effect. In addition, the price increase reduces the consumer's effective buying power. If the consumer were to buy the same quantity of the good, she would have less money to spend on other goods. This tends to decrease the amount of all goods the consumer purchases, including the one whose price has changed. This tendency is known as the income or wealth effect.

Substitution effects always decrease the quantity of a good that a consumer purchases, but the income effect can actually increase the quantity purchased. If the good whose price increases is already a lower quality but lower priced substitute for another good, then the loss of buying power might cause the consumer to purchase more of the lower quality good and to decrease her purchase of the higher priced, higher quality good. A good for which a decrease

---

[6] Technically it is possible for the amount of the good consumed to increase as price increases. A good for which this occurs is called a Giffen good. It is questionable whether there has ever been a true Giffen good in our modern economy. Whether or not such a good has ever existed, all economists would concede at least that they are extremely rare.

in income causes an increase in consumption is known as an inferior good. The traditional textbook candidate for an inferior good was margarine, a cheap but not so tasty substitute for butter. As the price of margarine increased, families could afford less butter and hence purchased more margarine. Whether or not margarine was ever an inferior good, the example does not work today because many consumers have avoided butter for health reasons, making margarine a preferred rather than inferior good.

Figure 6 depicts a graph illustrating the substitution and income effects. To generate Figure 6, we first reproduce our graph illustrating the effects of a price change on the overall consumption of the good. We then add to this a budget line parallel to that for the new prices, but tangent to the original indifference curve of the consumer prior to the price increase. The point of tangency on this hypothetical budget line represents the optimal consumption point that would result at the new price of the good if the consumer received a subsidy to bring her to the same level of utility that she originally enjoyed. The difference in quantity consumed due to the change in price, but keeping the consumer at his original lead of utility, results from the substitution effect. The remainder of the difference between the original and final quantity consumed results from the income effect.

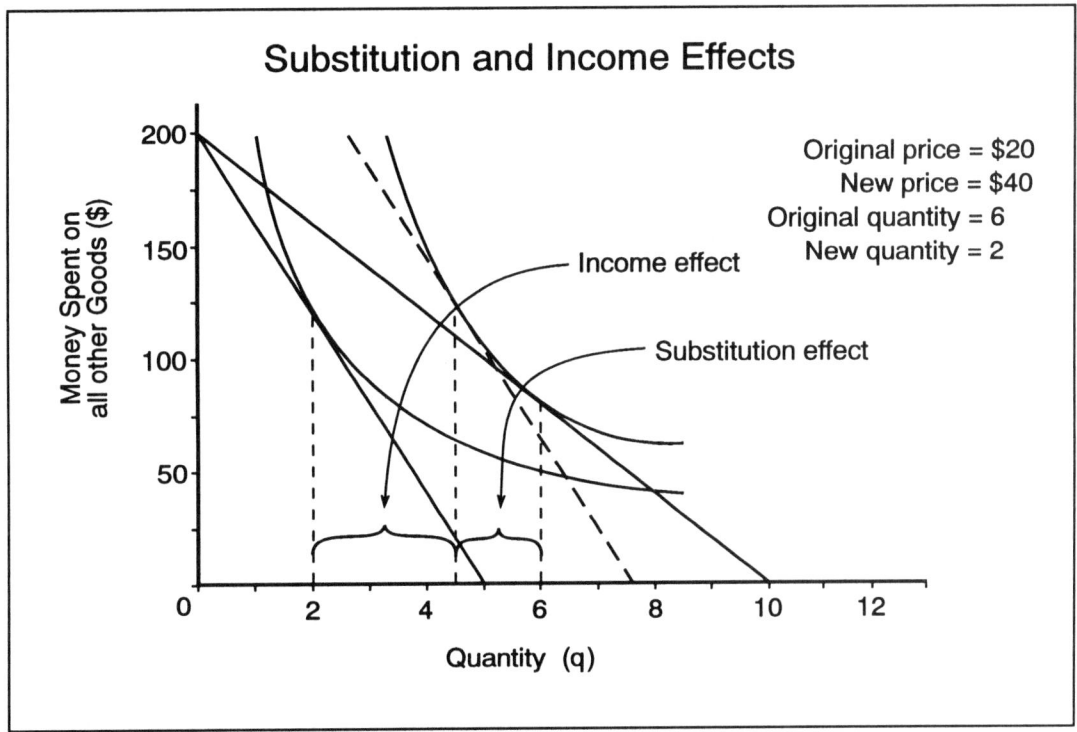

Figure 6

3. *Market demand*

Finally, we can use the techniques we have just learned to tie consumer choices to market demand. We begin by deriving a demand function for each individual. To do so, return to the graph that illustrates how Al's consumption changes with price changes for a good (Figure 5).

Notice that for each price, there is a unique budget curve **and a unique quantity that Al will purchase**. We can chart the relationship between the price for the good and the quantity that Al would purchase. This is Al's personal demand function. If we did this for every consumer in the relevant market, and added the quantity each demanded at a given price, we would get the demand function for the entire industry producing this good. If we graphed this function, we would have the industry demand curve.

Consider the following example of the demand for widgets in a three person society made up of Al, Barb, and Chris. Suppose the following table summarizes how many widgets each individual would purchase at any given price. Then summing the demand of all the individuals gives the total industry demand.

DEMAND FUNCTIONS FOR A THREE PERSON SOCIETY

PRICE	Q AL	Q BARB	Q CHRIS	Q TOTAL
$20	0	0	0	0
18	0	1	0	1
16	1	1	0	2
14	1	2	1	4
12	2	2	1	5
10	2	3	1	6
8	3	4	2	9
6	3	5	2	10
4	4	6	3	13
2	5	8	4	17

Figure 7 graphs these functions, showing the individual demand curves and summing them to show the industry demand curve.

4. *Elasticity of demand*

Market (or equivalently industry wide) demand curves are very useful because they allow the producer (or economist) to see how total quantity of consumption of a good will vary with price. This will allow firms in the industry to determine what will happen if they raise prices. The relationship of levels of consumption to price are so important that economists have defined a measure of how sensitive quantity is as a function of price, which they call price elasticity. (To distinguish this relationship for the demand curve from that for supply curves, economists actually define two measures, elasticity of supply and elasticity of demand. At this point we are concerned only with elasticity of demand, which we designate as η_D)

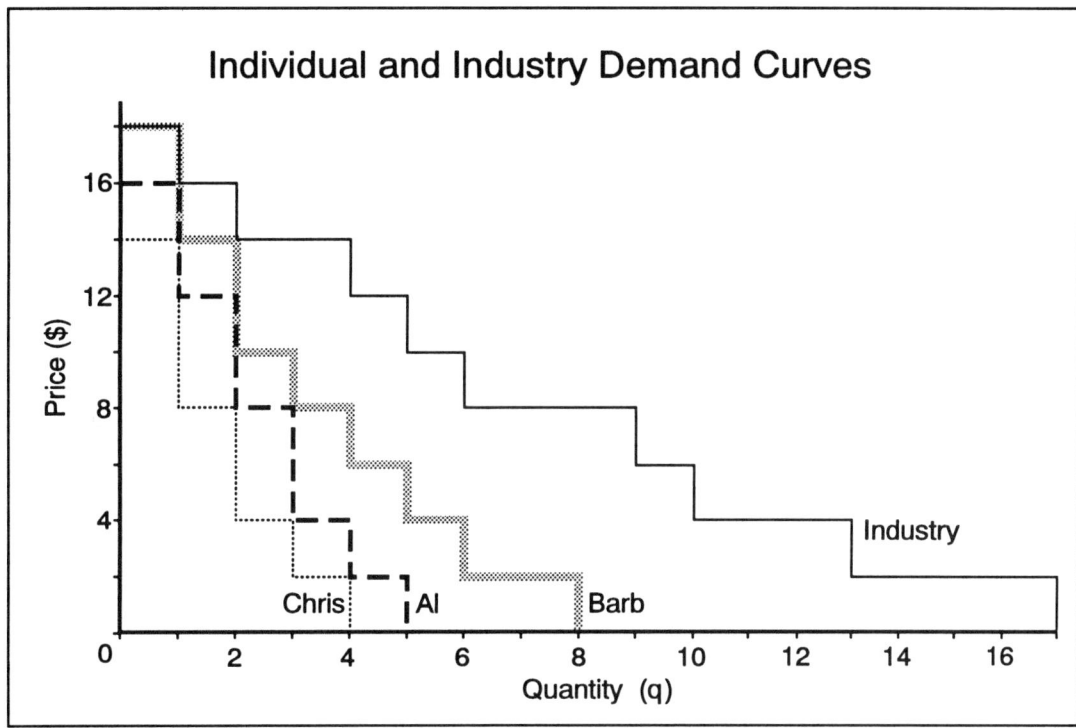

Figure 7

η_D is defined as the percentage change in quantity demanded divided by the percentage change in price that gave rise to the change in demand. In mathematical terms:

$$\eta_D = (\Delta Q/Q) \div (\Delta P/P)$$

Economists use percentage changes because such changes are a more meaningful measure of price sensitivity of demand than are absolute changes. Absolute changes in price almost always will have little effect on high priced goods but great effects on low priced goods. For example, a $.10 change in price cannot be expected to have the same effect on consumption of a good costing $20 as on one costing $.20.

A good for which a small percentage change in price causes a large percentage change in quantity demanded is called "elastic." A good for which a large percentage change in price causes only a small percentage change in quantity demanded is called "inelastic." One can get a rough feel for the elasticity of demand for a good from the shape of the demand curve; a good with a flat demand curve is elastic, while one with a steep demand curve is inelastic.

One attribute that we must recognize about elasticity is that it is sensitive to the time frame we are considering. For example, we may want to know how demand for home-heating oil will change over the next month if the price increases from $1.00 to $1.50. One would suspect that this would not cause a sharp decrease in demand over a month's time because individuals must keep warm, and those using home-heating oil have no choice but to buy what they need regardless of price. If, however, we wanted to know how the same increase would effect demand over the next ten years, we would expect a very different answer. Over that period of time, individuals could replace their oil furnaces with alternative forms of heating, for example using electricity or gas. Thus, over the longer period of time, consumers can adjust more easily to the increase in cost. Therefore, generally, long term elasticity of demand is greater than short term elasticity of demand. Figure 8 depicts a graph showing the general relationship between demand in the short and long run.

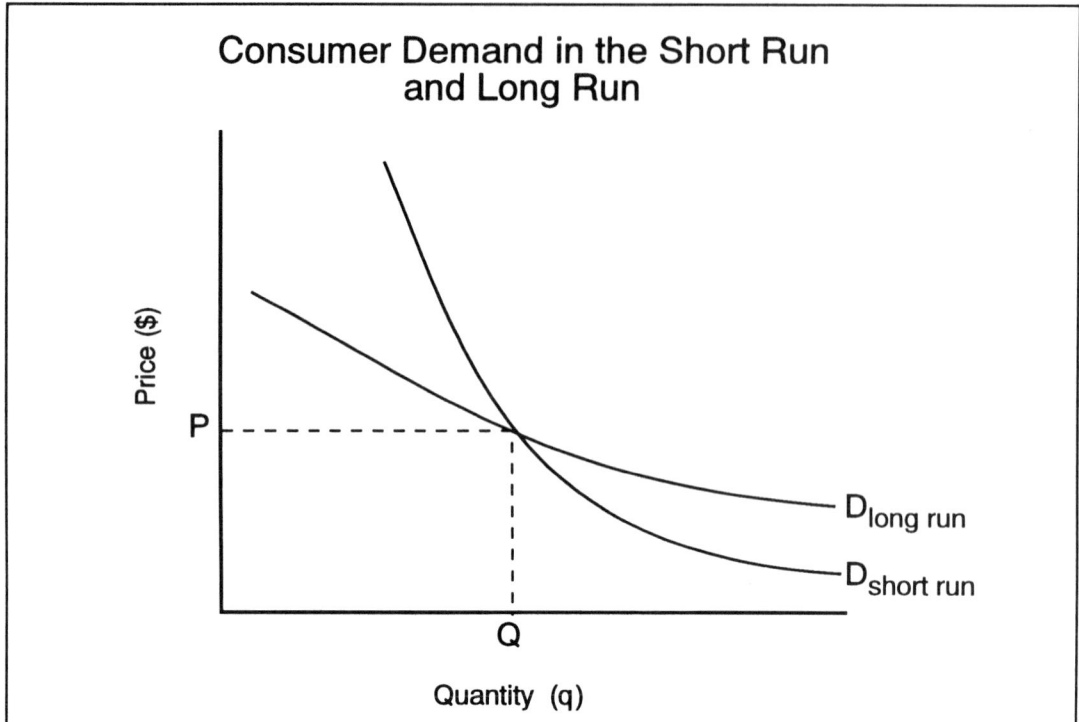

Figure 8

5. *Consumer surplus*

The final concept related to consumer choice is that of "consumer surplus." Consumer surplus is the excess value a consumer places on a good over the price of the good, or in other words, it is the effective increase in wealth a consumer realizes by making a voluntary purchase. A simple example illustrates the concept. Suppose that Joe Student finds a book that would really help him as a reference tool. He would be willing to pay $40 for the book. Fortunately for Joe, the price of the book is only $32. If Joe buys the book he is $8 better off than before the purchase. He has given up the opportunity to use the $32 to purchase other goods, but has gotten something that he values at $40! The difference between his subjective valuation of the book and the price he pays, in this case $8, is the consumer surplus generated by the transaction.

We can relate consumer surplus to the demand curves we just generated. Refer back to Al's demand function in our three person society. Al would be willing to buy one widget for $16, but none if the price were above that. Hence, the value of that widget to Al must be $16. He would be willing to buy a second widget for $12, but not for any price above that. Hence, the value of the second widget to Al is $12. By continuing this reasoning, we see that Al's demand curve graphs the value he places on each additional widget. If the actual price of widgets is known, that price can be graphed on the same curve as a horizontal line. The area under Al's demand curve and above the price line then represents the consumer surplus Al derives from purchasing the number of widgets he desires at the given price. One can draw a price line on the industry demand curve as well, and the area between the demand curve and the price line then represents the total consumer surplus for all individuals in society. Figure 9 graphically illustrates the concept of consumer surplus.

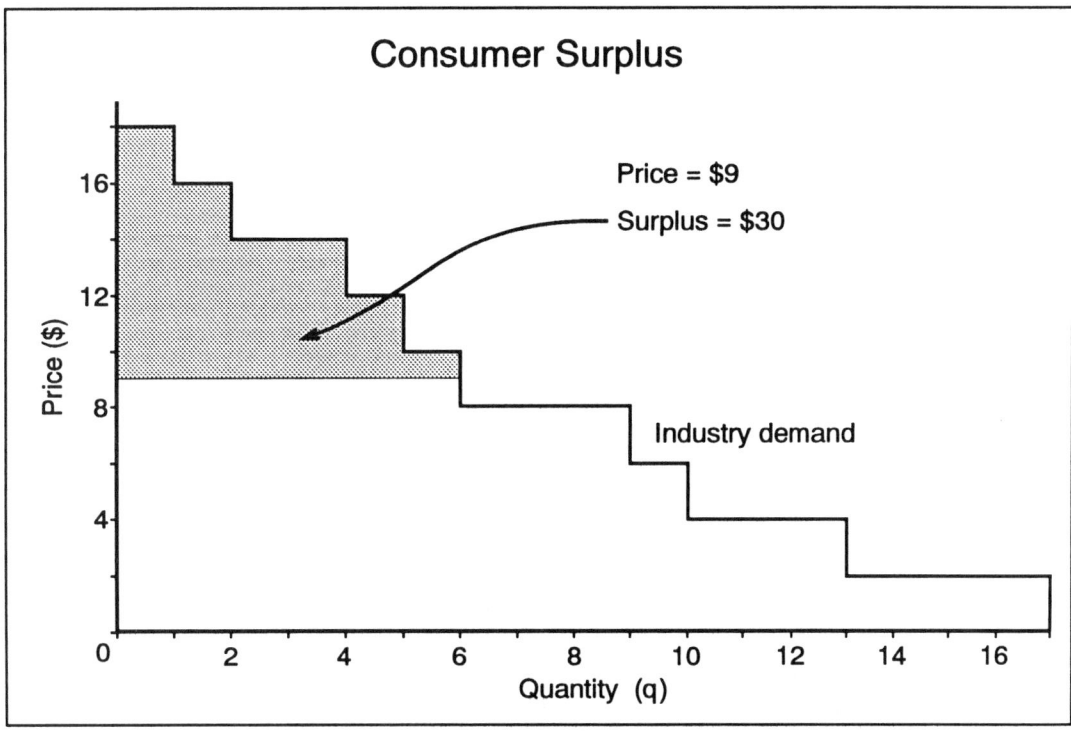

Figure 9

6. *Using indifference curves and budget lines to answer economic questions—an example*

Generally, economists and governmental actors do not know the preference functions of individuals for government provided goods such as legal rules. There are no markets for such goods, so economists try to derive the preferences from studies of "shadow markets" in which parties alter the effects of legal rules privately. Even without knowing consumer preferences, however, the theory of indifference curves and budget lines is helpful because it clarifies the assumptions that underlie demand curves and analyses of economic transactions between consumers. Moreover, the theory can help answer some questions even if we do not know consumers' underlying preference functions.

Consider a northern city just after a sharp rise of home-heating oil prices from $1.00 to $1.50 per gallon. Poor people in the city feel the pinch more extremely than others; some

18   MICROECONOMIC PREDICATES TO LAW AND ECONOMICS

families have no money to pay for sufficient heat to keep their apartments at a livable temperature. The average poor family paid $1000 a year for heating oil at the old prices. To alleviate the hardship of these people, the city is thinking of giving them a lump sum payment of $500 for the year to offset the increased cost of the oil. The City Counsel would like to know whether, after the increase in home-heating oil prices **and with the subsidy**, the indigent families are better off, worse off or equally well off as they were before the increase in price. (The City Counsel is not concerned with making up for any possible increases in the price of other goods). Our theory of consumer choice allows us to answer this question.

The solution is presented in Figure 10. We start by drawing a poor family's budget line for the original price of $1.00 per gallon on a graph with home-heating oil on the X-axis and all other goods on the Y-axis. We then draw a representative indifference curve tangent to the budget line. (We do not need to know the precise shape of these curves to answer the questions above.) The point of tangency represents the family's optimal consumption of oil and other goods at the original price of oil. We can now draw a second budget line which represents the mix of goods that the family can buy after the price change and the lump sum payment. The slope of that line will be $3/2$ the slope of the original budget line. It will also pass through the original optimal point because the City will be giving the family just enough money to allow it to buy the same amount of oil as it did before the price increase without the family having to give up any purchase of other goods.

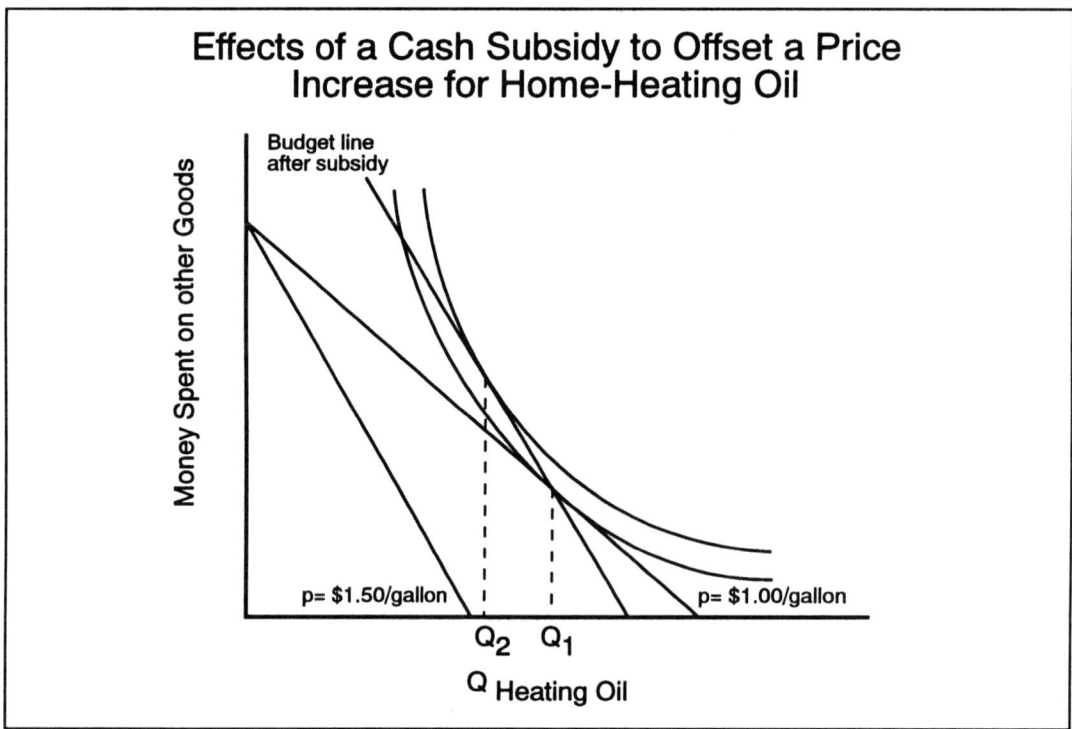

Figure 10

The graph in Figure 10 demonstrates that the family will be better off after the price increase and the subsidy (assuming all other prices remain constant). The family can reach its original consumption point, so we know it cannot be worse off. But now, because the relative prices of goods has changed, this is not the family's optimal point. It can reach an even higher indifference curve by giving up the purchase of some oil, **now saving $1.50 per gallon by doing so**, and using the money saved to buy goods it values more than oil at this new, higher price.

Suggested Additional Reading

Robert C. Ellickson, *Bringing Culture and Human Frailty to Rational Actors: A Critique of Classical Law and Economics*, 65 CHI-KENT L. REV. 23 (1989).

Milton Friedman, *The Marshallian Demand Curve*, in Milton Friedman, ESSAYS IN POSITIVE ECONOMICS 47-99 (1953).

Edwin Mansfield, MICROECONOMICS: THEORY AND APPLICATIONS 53-140 (8th ed. 1994).

Richard H. McAdams, *Relative Preferences*, 102 YALE L.J. 1 (1992).

Richard Thaler, *Toward a Positive Theory of Consumer Choice*, 1 J. ECON. BEHAVIOR & ORG. 39 (1980).

2
Producer Decisions—Cost, Revenue and Profit Maximization

Having looked at the consumer side of the market, we turn our attention to the producer side. As for consumers, economists posit a model of producer behavior. Specifically, they assume that producers act to maximize their profits. Using this model, economists are able to predict how producers would behave in a number of idealized market settings, such as purely competitive markets and pure monopolies.

Profit is the economic benefit a producer obtains from producing and selling a good. It is simply the difference between the producer's revenues from sales and the producer's costs of production and sale. Thus, one component of profit is cost. Our first concern will be to understand the costs facing a producer of a particular good. In particular we need to know what those costs represent, and how a producer uses cost to decide how much of a good to produce and how to price the goods it produces.

A. Producers' Cost Functions

1. *Opportunity cost*

Producers face costs because they have to devote resources to the production of their goods. Such resources include the raw materials from which goods are made, the labor of the employees who manufacture and sell the goods, and machines and plants used to produce the goods. Use of such resources is costly because a producer using them denies their use by others. In other words, the producer denies the opportunity for these resources to be used to produce other goods. Ultimately, a producer will incur out of pocket expenses because the producer is competing with others seeking to put the resources to other uses. The notion of economic cost, however, is not the out of pocket expenses that the producer incurs. Rather, economic cost is the value lost by preventing the resources from being used to produce other goods. This is called "opportunity cost" to distinguish it from ordinary notions of cost, which economists call accounting cost.

Economists use opportunity cost because it allows them implicitly to compare uses for resources without having to specify explicitly the value of the resources if put to another use. Thus, when a producer calculates its profit it inherently takes into account the money it could make from producing alternative goods. So long as use of resources increases the profit of a producer calculated using economic (*i.e.* opportunity) cost then the producer knows that it is not giving up a greater profit that it could earn by devoting those resources to other ventures.

The economic notion of cost is extremely important, and it is worth our while to become comfortable with that notion. Therefore, let's look at an example that illustrates the type of costs that must be included in a calculation of opportunity cost.

Suppose Josephine is considering going to law school. Tuition and books for law school cost $15,000 per year. (Assume these are paid at the beginning of the year.) Currently Josephine works in an office earning $10 per hour. (Ignore income tax for the sake of simplicity.) She works 40 hours a week, 50 weeks of the year, and therefore receives total pay of $20,000 per year. (For the sake of simplicity, assume that Josephine would receive the entire pay at the end of the year.) Josephine could earn $15 an hour for overtime, but she chooses not to, preferring to have some leisure time. Josephine, however, expects to take law school very seriously and therefore to work 50 hours a week on her studies. (Make one final simplifying assumption—that Josephine expects to work on her law studies for a full 50 weeks during the year.) What is Josephine's economic cost of attending law school?

Her out of pocket costs are $15,000 per year. She also loses the opportunity to invest this money and earn a return on it. Assuming she could invest it at 10% in a venture about as risky as her legal career, by spending the money on law school she forgoes the opportunity to earn another $1,500 each year. In addition, Josephine devotes her labor to law studies, which deprives her of the opportunity to earn $20,000. Finally, Josephine also devotes 10 extra hours a week to law school. Although we may not know exactly how much she values this time, we know she values it at more than $15 per hour, because she has already given up the opportunity to work for this amount in order to have more leisure time. Over the 50 weeks, she gives up leisure that is worth at least $7,500 to her (10 hours per week x 50 weeks x $15 per hour). Thus, Josephine's opportunity cost of law school is at least $44,000 per year.

2. *Efficient use of resources and the total cost function*

With this understanding of cost under our belts, we wish to develop a theory of producer decision-making akin to that for consumers. To do so, we must conduct our analysis somewhat backwards. We first act as though the producer knows how much of the good it wants to produce, and then we determine how the producer will employ various inputs to produce that quantity. Knowing how the producer would employ inputs, we can calculate a cost for every level of production—the producer's total cost function. Once we have this cost function, we posit that producers will maximize profits. We then use this supposition to determine how much of the good the producer will actually manufacture.

Producers must purchase inputs to produce their products. For example, a shoe manufacturer must purchase machinery, leather, and workers to operate the machinery. Most likely the manufacturer will have to purchase or rent space for office workers to keep track of orders, to ship the product, etc. As we did for the theory of consumer choice, however, we can assume that production involves only two inputs without changing any of the ideas that flow from the analysis. So let's assume that our shoe manufacturer has to decide how much labor (L) and capital (K) it must use to produce a specific quantity of shoes, say 1000 pairs.

We begin our analysis by creating a graph with capital on one axis and labor on the other. We then connect all the points representing levels of capital and labor that can be used to produce 1000 pairs of shoes. This curve is known as an isoquant or curve of constant output. Production processes generally exhibit diminishing marginal productivity. That is, if the producer keeps capital fixed as it adds labor, the amount of additional product it can produce from adding one more unit of labor decreases. For this reason, isoquants, like preference curves, will be convex to the origin. Unlike preference curves, however, isoquants can curve back on themselves: for a fixed amount of capital one may add so much labor that workers interfere with one another and the quantity produced goes down. Of course in this curl back region the producer is paying for labor and capital that actually decreases output. Since greater output means greater revenue, a profit maximizing producer will never operate in the curl back region. Hence, we can simply ignore this region. The remaining area, in which a producer might operate, is known as the production region. The graph in Figure 11 shows a set of isoquants for various levels of shoe production and identifies the production and curl back regions.

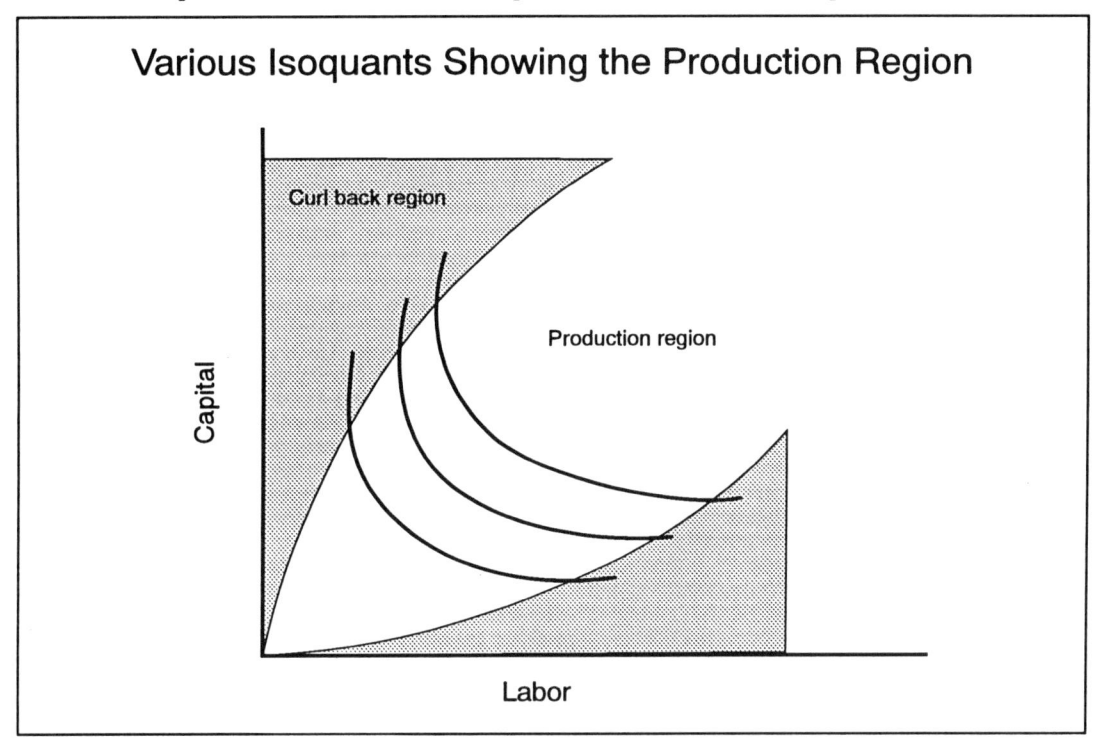

Various Isoquants Showing the Production Region

Figure 11

Once we specify how a producer can utilize capital and labor to produce a set quantity of shoes, we must consider the costs of production. Each point in the production region represents a quantity of capital and labor. We presume that the producer must pay the "going" price for capital and labor. Hence, we can assign a cost to each point according to the following equation:

$$C = p_K \cdot K + p_L \cdot L$$

If we solve for K in terms of L, we get the equation for a straight line with a negative slope of p_L/p_K and a y-intercept of C/p_K. We can graph these "isocost" lines on the same graph as our isoquant for various values of C. By moving along the isoquant, we can determine the efficient levels of capital and labor—the levels that minimize the costs of producing 1000 pairs of shoes. These levels correspond to the point at which the isoquant touches the lowest isocost curve with which it intersects, which will occur at the point where the isoquant is tangent to an isocost line. This is shown in Figure 12.

Efficient Mix of Labor and Capital to Produce 1000 Pairs of Shoes

[Figure: Graph with Capital on vertical axis and Labor on horizontal axis. Four parallel isocost lines labeled C_1, C_2, C_3, C_4 (from lowest to highest) intersect with an isoquant curve representing 1000 pairs of shoes. The isoquant is tangent to the C_2 isocost line, indicating the minimum cost of producing 1000 pairs of shoes equals C_2.]

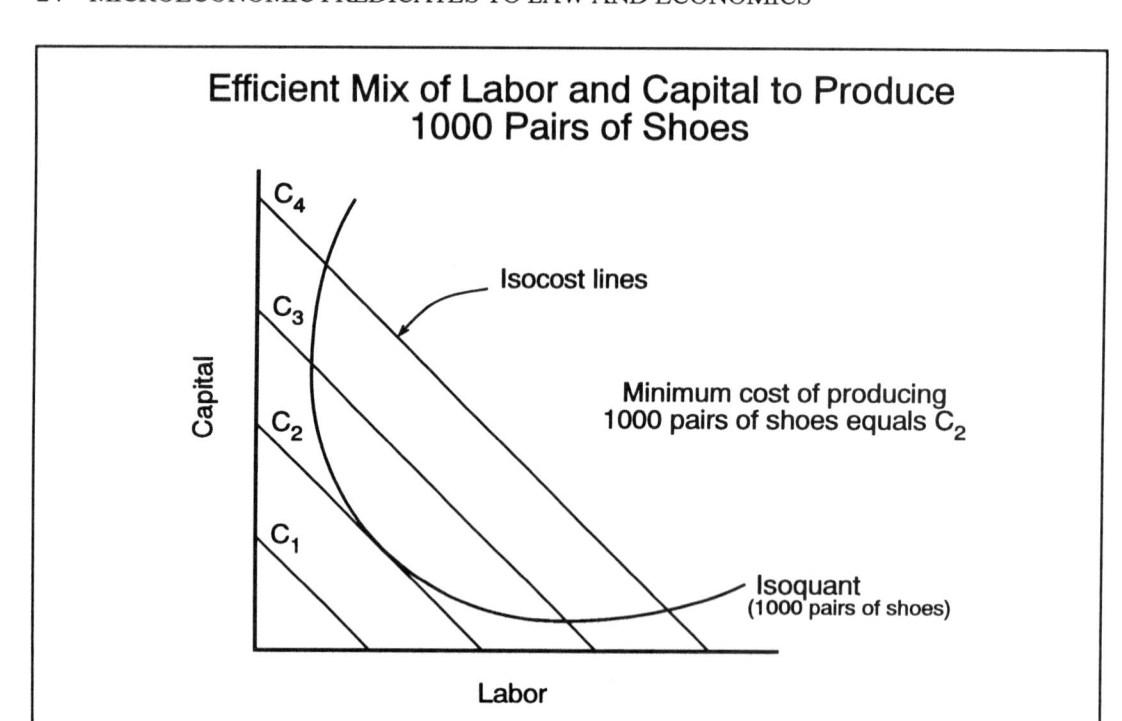

Figure 12

By repeating this procedure for different levels of production, a producer can determine not only the best level of capital and labor to use for each quantity it might want to produce, but also the minimum cost it will incur for producing at each level of output. This is illustrated in Figure 13. For each quantity there will be a minimal cost of production, and this minimum cost at each quantity is the producer's total cost function. This is denoted as $C(Q)$ to show that the cost is a function of the quantity produced. The construction of this function makes it evident that the cost function is the cost the producer experiences assuming it uses inputs (*e.g.* capital and labor) in the most efficient manner.

3. *Marginal cost and average cost, and their relationship to total cost*

Producers often find it easier to focus on per unit costs rather than aggregate costs. There are two different measures of per unit cost that producers use for different purposes: average cost and marginal cost. Average cost is just total cost divided by total quantity. Marginal cost is the increase in cost necessary to produce one additional unit of output. More generally, when output is measured in continuous units (such as when measuring volumes of a liquid), marginal cost is defined as the additional cost incurred to produce a slightly increased output divided by the increase in output. We can express both of these entities mathematically:

Cost as a Function of Output

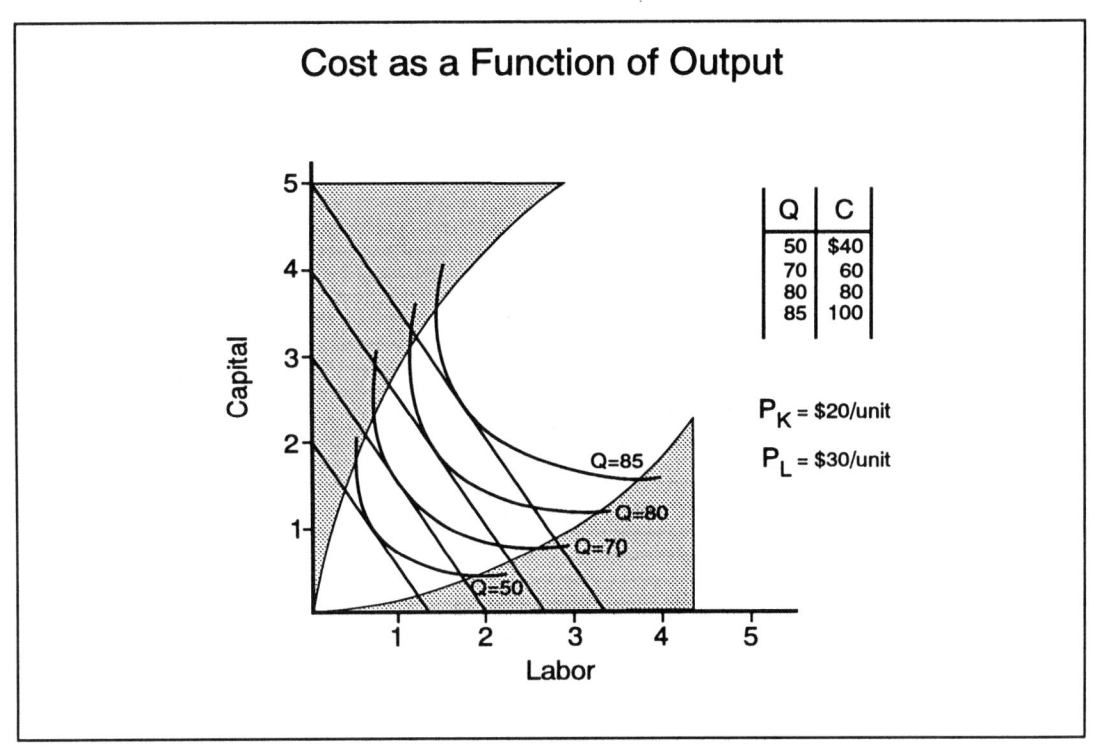

Figure 13

Q	C
50	$40
70	60
80	80
85	100

P_K = $20/unit
P_L = $30/unit

$$\text{Average Cost (A.C.)} = \text{Total Cost } (C(Q)) \div \text{Quantity } (Q)$$

$$\text{Marginal Cost (M.C.)} = [C(Q) - C(Q-1)]$$
or equivalently
$$\text{Marginal Cost} = [C(Q) - C(Q-\Delta Q)] \div \Delta Q$$

There are several interesting relationships between total cost, average cost and marginal cost. First, given a complete specification of any one of these functions, we can derive the other two. We have specified how to derive average cost and marginal cost from total cost in the equations above. Total cost at quantity Q can be derived from average cost simply by multiplying A.C.(Q) by Q. Total cost can be derived from marginal cost by summing the marginal cost for all quantities less than and equal to Q. That is:

$$C(Q) = M.C.(1) + M.C.(2) + \ldots + M.C.(Q-1) + M.C.(Q).$$

Additionally, if we graph the total cost function, the average cost at any quantity is the slope of the ray from the origin to the point on the curve representing the cost at that quantity. Also, the marginal cost at any quantity is the slope of the tangent to the total cost curve at that quantity. These geometric properties of average and marginal cost follow directly from the definitions of total, average and marginal cost, as Figure 14 illustrates.

Geometric Relationship Between Total Cost, Average Cost and Marginal Cost

Marginal cost at any quantity, Q, is the slope of the tangent to the total cost curve at Q.

Average cost at any quantity, Q, is the slope of the ray from the origin to the total cost revenue at Q.

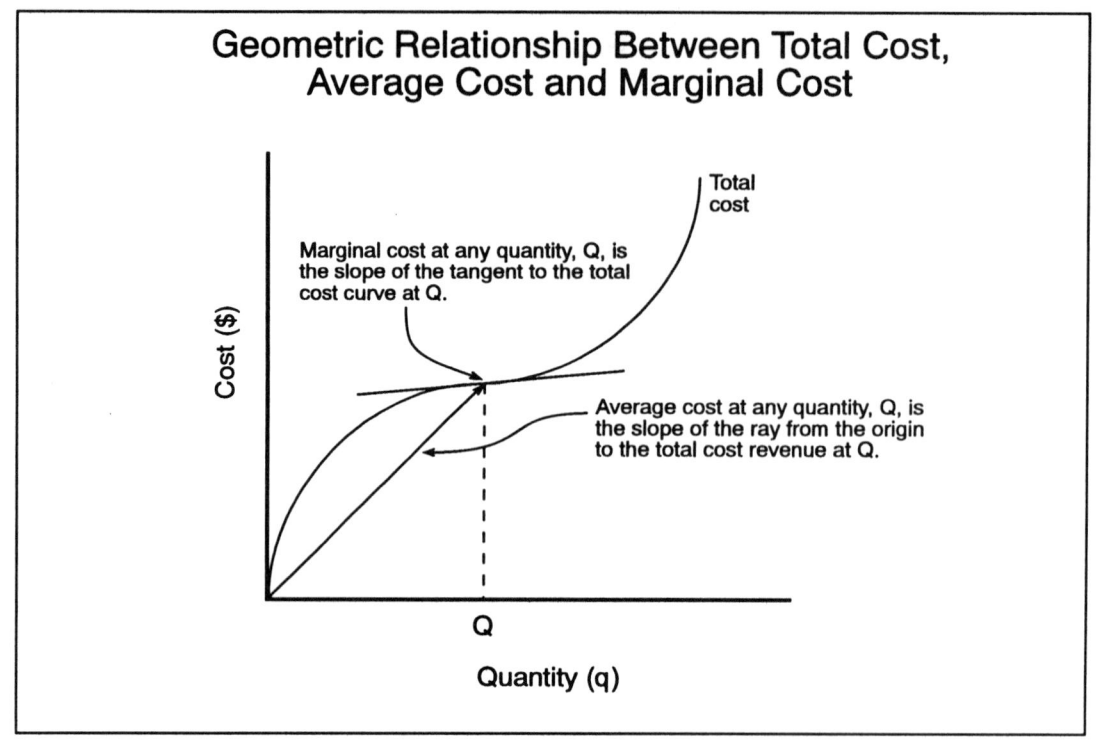

Figure 14

A final relationship, which is of great significance for the economics of competitive markets, is that the point at which the average cost curve crosses the marginal cost curve is the minimum value of the average cost curve. There are several ways to understand why this is so. The average cost at Q can be calculated by averaging the marginal cost at Q into the average cost at Q-1. Prior to the point at which the curves cross, marginal cost is less than an average cost. Including a number that is less than an existing average into a new average will necessarily pull the new average down. Thus, the new average will continue to drop until the marginal cost rises to a level at which it is no longer below average cost (i.e. the point at which the values are equal). Graphically one can demonstrate the relationship by noting that the ray from the origin to the total cost curve has its least slope when that ray is a tangent to the total cost curve. But, by the relationship between the total and marginal cost curves, that is precisely when the slope is also the marginal cost at that point. The relationship between average cost and marginal cost is illustrated in Figures 15 and 16, which graph total cost and per unit cost respectively.

Average Cost Equals Marginal Cost at the Point Where Average Cost is a Minimum

At Q_m the slope of the ray from the origin to the total cost curve is a minimum.

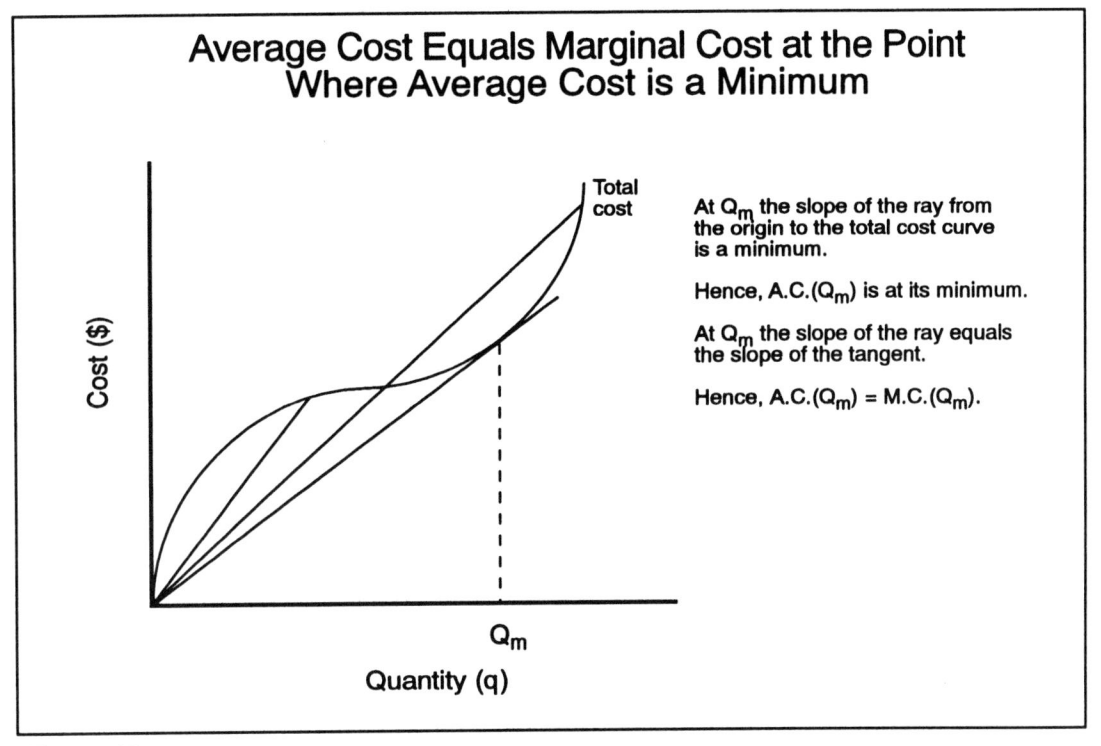

Hence, $A.C.(Q_m)$ is at its minimum.

At Q_m the slope of the ray equals the slope of the tangent.

Hence, $A.C.(Q_m) = M.C.(Q_m)$.

Figure 15

The Average Cost Curve Crosses the Marginal Cost at the Point Where Average Cost is a Minimum

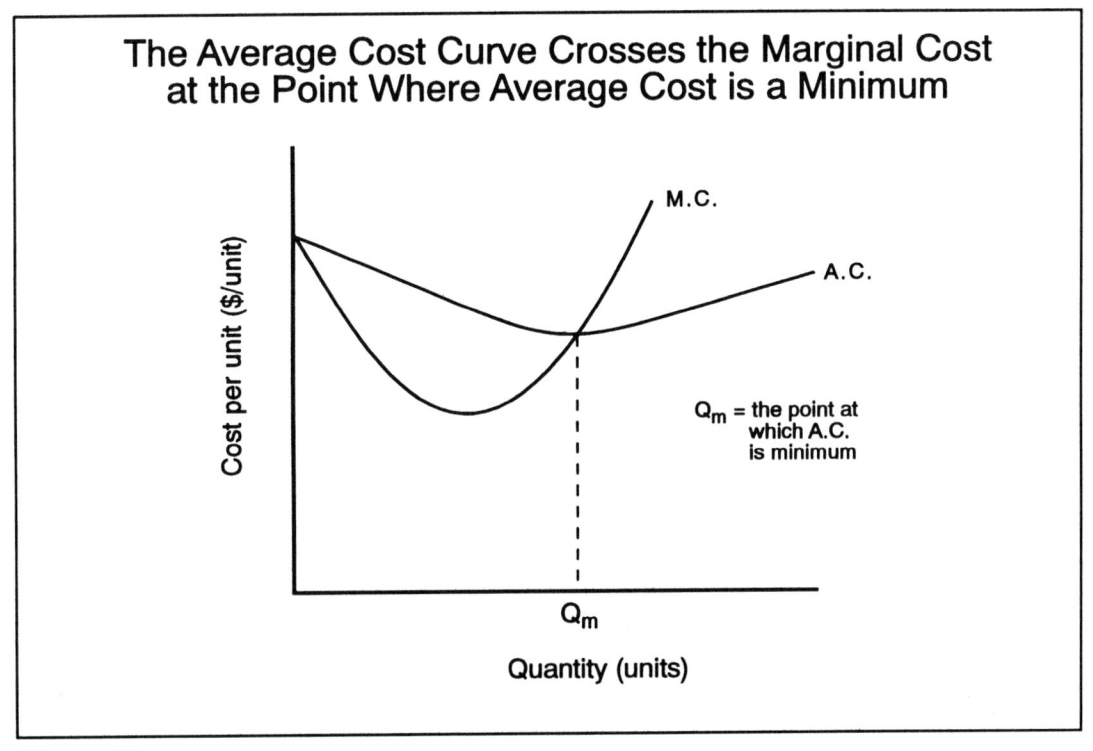

Q_m = the point at which A.C. is minimum

Figure 16

4. *Fixed costs and variable costs*

The final concept related to costs that we will need to understand is the difference between fixed and variable costs. Remember that costs arise because the producer must pay for inputs to production. A cost is considered to be fixed if it results from use of an input whose quantity cannot be altered in the period of time being considered by the firm. A cost is considered to be variable if it results from use of an input whose quantity can be changed during the relevant period. Fixed costs tend to include depreciation for capital items such as the plant and large pieces of machinery. Variable costs tend to include the costs of labor and raw materials. But these characterizations are not always accurate. On the one hand, sometimes the producer can easily sell existing machinery in a short period of time, and the decision not to do so may create variable costs (remember costs are opportunity costs). On the other hand, sometimes a firm has committed to purchasing set quantities of labor and raw materials via long term contracts, in which case it cannot avoid the costs of these inputs. The key distinction between fixed and variable costs is that the former will not change with levels of production and that the latter will.

The relevant period for determining whether a cost is variable or fixed will vary depending on the nature of the decision facing the firm. A firm facing a decision whether to increase its production by adding a graveyard shift is considering a decision in which the time horizon is not so long that the firm will be replacing its plant or machinery. A firm deciding whether to enter into a business at all, before it commits to plant, machinery and labor costs, is obviously considering a time horizon during which the size of its plant and its investment in machinery will vary.

Related to the concepts of fixed and variable costs are those of the short and long run time horizons. The long run is a period of time over which **all** inputs are variable. This means that over the long run the firm can vary the size of its plant, the amount of equipment it buys, etc. The short run is any period for which some of the firm's inputs are fixed. Even in the short run, a firm will have the flexibility to vary many inputs. But the firm will be committed to a level of at least some inputs (usually plant and equipment) over the short run. Thus, firms have greater flexibility to vary their inputs to production over the long run than they do over the short run.

B. Producers' Decisions: Profit Maximization and the Level of Production

1. *The meaning of economic profit*

As noted at the beginning of this chapter, a firm will choose the level of production that maximizes its profits. Economic profit is defined as the revenue (R) the firm derives from the production and sale of its goods minus the firm's economic total cost of production and sale. It is important to remember, however, that economic cost is opportunity cost. Thus, if a producer earns a 10% return on an initial investment in capital and labor his profit may not be 10%. If he could have earned 8% by using his money in some other venture, his actual profit would only be 2%. In other words, a firm does not make economic profit just because it makes money in an accounting sense. It makes an economic profit only if its return is greater than the expected return for other investments involving similar risk.

There is special significance to economic profit that is exactly zero. Because economists define costs as opportunity costs, a firm that earns a positive profit is earning more money than it could if it had used its resources in alternative ventures. Similarly, a firm that is making a negative economic profit is making less money than it would have had it invested in other ventures. Hence, a firm that earns a zero economic profit is doing just as well as it would have had it invested in other ventures. For that reason, we say a firm earning a zero economic profit is earning a "normal return" on its investment. Note, that a firm that is earning a negative economic profit may be earning money, and hence showing a positive profit in the accounting sense; it just is not earning as much as it would have had it gone into a different business.

2. *Choosing the level of production that maximizes profit: the relationship of marginal revenue and marginal cost to profit maximization*

A firm maximizes its profit by producing a quantity for which total revenue exceeds total cost by the greatest amount possible. Firms may find it easier, however, to decide how much of a good to produce by using the concepts of marginal revenue and marginal cost. The marginal revenue at a quantity Q is the increase in revenue a producer can obtain by producing Q units instead of Q-1 units of a good. In arithmetic terms:

$$M.R.(Q) = R(Q) - R(Q-1)$$

To maximize profits a firm should continue to produce an additional unit so long as marginal revenue for the unit is greater than marginal cost of that unit. As long as that is the case, the firm derives a positive economic profit by producing that unit. A firm should not produce an additional unit for which marginal cost exceeds marginal revenue, as production of that unit will cause a negative profit—that is, it will result in a decrease in the net profit. From the preceding two statements it follows that a firm should continue producing additional quantities of a good until it produces the precise quantity at which marginal revenue equals marginal cost.

The analysis of profit in terms of marginal revenue and cost also allows us to represent profits graphically. The profit the firm derives from each unit it produces and sells is the difference between the marginal revenue and marginal cost for that unit. Graphically this is the rectangular area between the marginal revenue curve and the marginal cost curve for that unit. The firm's total profit can be found by summing the profit derived from producing each unit. This is just the sum of the rectangles between the marginal revenue and marginal cost curves, which in turn is the total area between these two curves. (One must remember, however, that at any level of production for which marginal cost exceeds marginal revenue, the profit is negative, and this part of the area between the curves must be subtracted from the area where marginal revenue exceeds marginal cost.) Figure 17 illustrates how total profit can be represented by the areas between the marginal revenue and marginal cost curves.

3. *Deciding whether to enter into a business: the relationship between price, average cost and economic profit*

We can represent profit more easily on a graph that shows average cost. From the definition that sells every unit it produces at a single price, revenue equals the price multiplied by the quantity produced. Therefore:

$$\text{Profit } (\Pi) = R - T.C. = (P - A.C.) \cdot Q$$

Profit Represented in Terms of the Areas Between the Marginal Cost and Marginal Cost Revenue Curves

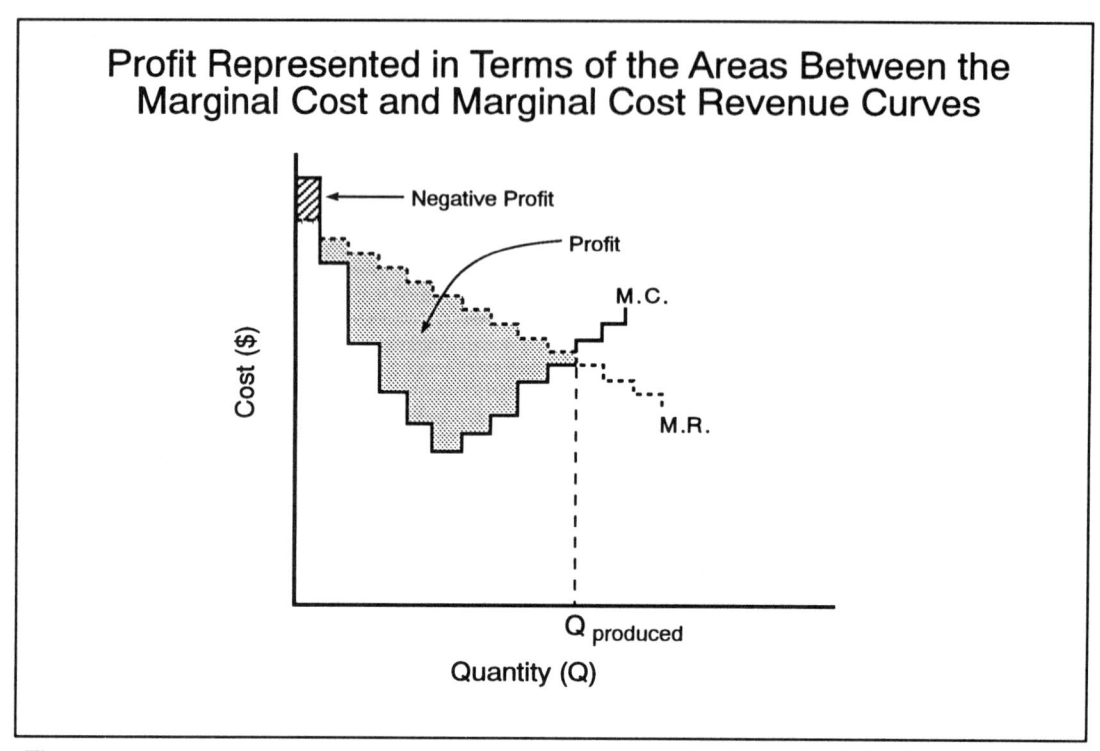

Figure 17

In other words, profit can be represented graphically as the area of the rectangle of width Q and height (P - A.C.), and will be positive as long as P > A.C. The relationship between the profit-maximizing operating level for the producer, its profit, and its marginal and average cost is shown in Figure 18.

If a firm produces at the profit maximizing quantity, it still might not make a positive profit. A negative profit means that the firm's average cost is greater than the price it can get for its goods. In that case, if the firm has not yet committed resources to the business, the firm should not go into that business at all, as it could make more money investing in other ventures![7]

---

[7] A firm that has a negative profit that has already invested in a business may still be best off continuing in that business, because the owners may not be able to recoup their entire investment if they decide to shut down and go into other ventures. If a profit maximizing firm faces prices that are lower than its average *variable* cost, it should shut down immediately, as each unit that the firm is producing is costing the firm more than it gets by producing and selling the unit.

Relationship of Profit to Marginal and Average Cost

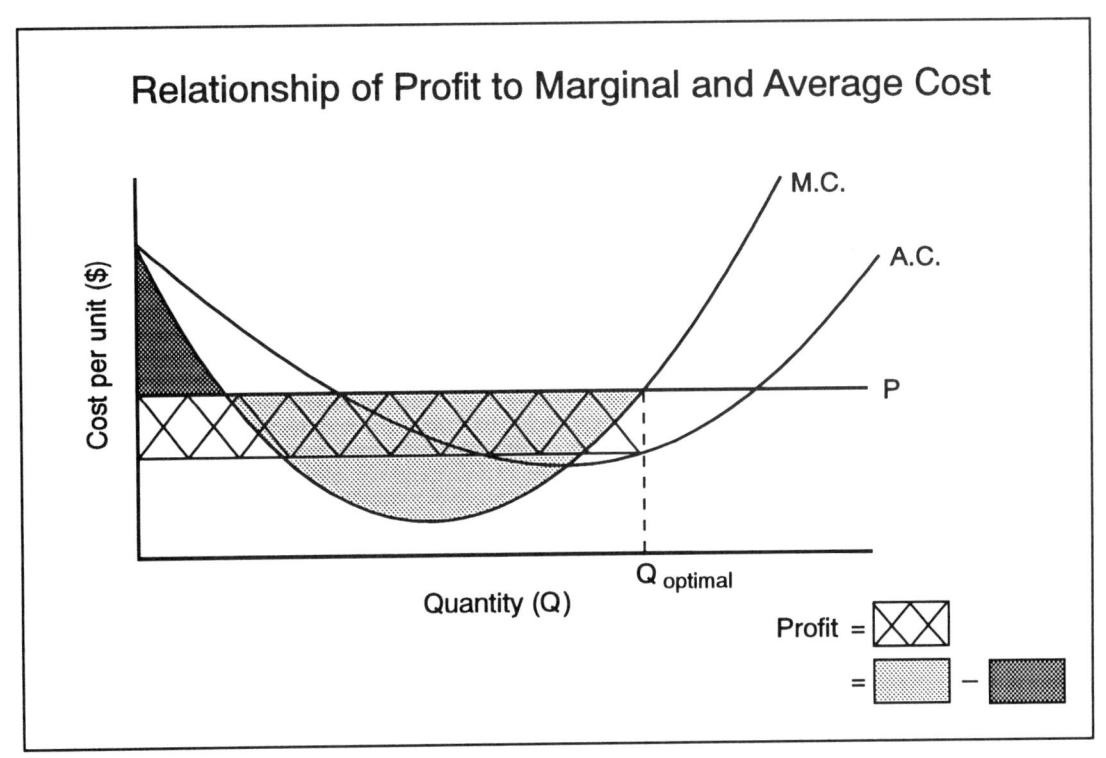

[Figure 18: Graph showing M.C. (Marginal Cost) and A.C. (Average Cost) curves with price line P, Q optimal marked on Quantity (Q) axis, Cost per unit ($) on vertical axis. Profit = cross-hatched area = shaded rectangle − dark triangle.]

Figure 18

4. Choosing the profit maximizing level of production of shoes given a cost function—an example

We have seen that a firm's revenue and cost functions allow it to determine what level of output will maximize its profits. A producer's revenue function, however, will depend on the market in which the producer operates. Until we introduce more information about the structures of such markets, we cannot specify in detail how the producer should go about determining its optimal level of output. We can, however, illustrate how a firm should go about choosing a level of production that maximizes profit if we make certain assumptions about how its level of production will affect the price of the good it produces. The following problem does just that.

Suppose a company is considering going into business manufacturing shoes. It has a choice between two machines. The first is cheaper to buy but more expensive to operate. The second is more expensive to buy but less expensive to operate. Both machines get more expensive to operate as they produce more shoes. The following table gives all the cost information for each machine.

32   MICROECONOMIC PREDICATES TO LAW AND ECONOMICS

Machine #	Cost of Machine	Cost of Prod. Each Pr. (For Pairs 1-100)	Cost of Prod. Each Pr. (For Pairs 101-200)	Cost of Prod. Each Pr. (For Pairs 201-300)
1	$1500	$30	$50	$70
2	$4000	$ 5	$25	$45

Assume as well that the price for shoes is $40 per pair and that the introduction of the company's shoes onto the market will not affect this price. How many shoes should the company produce?

We begin by generating a cost curve for shoe production. Remember that the cost curve represents the cost of producing given quantities of shoes at least cost. Hence, for each quantity that the company might produce, we must first determine which machine is the least cost means of production. We can do this by graphing the total costs incurred using each machine, and noting at any particular quantity which curve is lower. Figure 19 contains this graph. The graph demonstrates that for quantities of 1 to 100 pairs of shoes, machine 1 is the cheapest means of production; for quantities of 100 or more pairs of shoes, machine 2 is the cheapest means of production.[8]

We can now graph the marginal cost curve for shoe production. For Q = 1, the marginal cost is the total cost of producing the first pair, which is $1530. For Q = 2 through 100, the cost of each additional pair of shoes is $30. (Remember, we would purchase and use machine 1 to produce this number of pairs.) Hence the marginal cost for these quantities is $30. For Q =101 to 200 we can deduce by an identical process that the marginal cost is $25. (Remember that for this level of production we would purchase and use machine 2). Finally, for Q=201 to 300, the marginal cost is $45. This is shown on Figure 20.

---

[8] One could have determined this algebraically instead of graphically. It is easy to see that machine 1 is the cheapest means of producing 1 pair of shoes: the cost using machine 1 to produce one pair of shoes is $1530 while the cost using machine 2 is $4005. We would like to see if there is a quantity at which the total cost using machine 1 and that using machine 2 cross. If there is, we can surmise that machine 2 is the cheaper means of producing quantities greater than this cross-over quantity.

If there is a quantity at which the two curves cross, the costs using each machine must be the same at this quantity. We can thus solve for such a point by setting the total costs using each machine equal and seeing if any value of Q satisfies the equation. The equation is:

$$\$1500 + \$30 \cdot Q = \$4000 + \$5 \cdot Q \quad (0 \leq Q \leq 100).$$

(Note, if Q turns out to be greater than 100, we will have to write a new equation representing the costs of using each machine for greater levels of production.) This equation is satisfied for Q=100. Hence, machine 1 is the cheapest means of producing up to 100 pairs of shoes, and machine 2 is the cheapest means of producing more than 100 pairs of shoes.

PRODUCER DECISIONS—COST, REVENUE AND PROFIT MAXIMIZATION

Total Cost of Producing Shoes Using Machine 1 and Using Machine 2

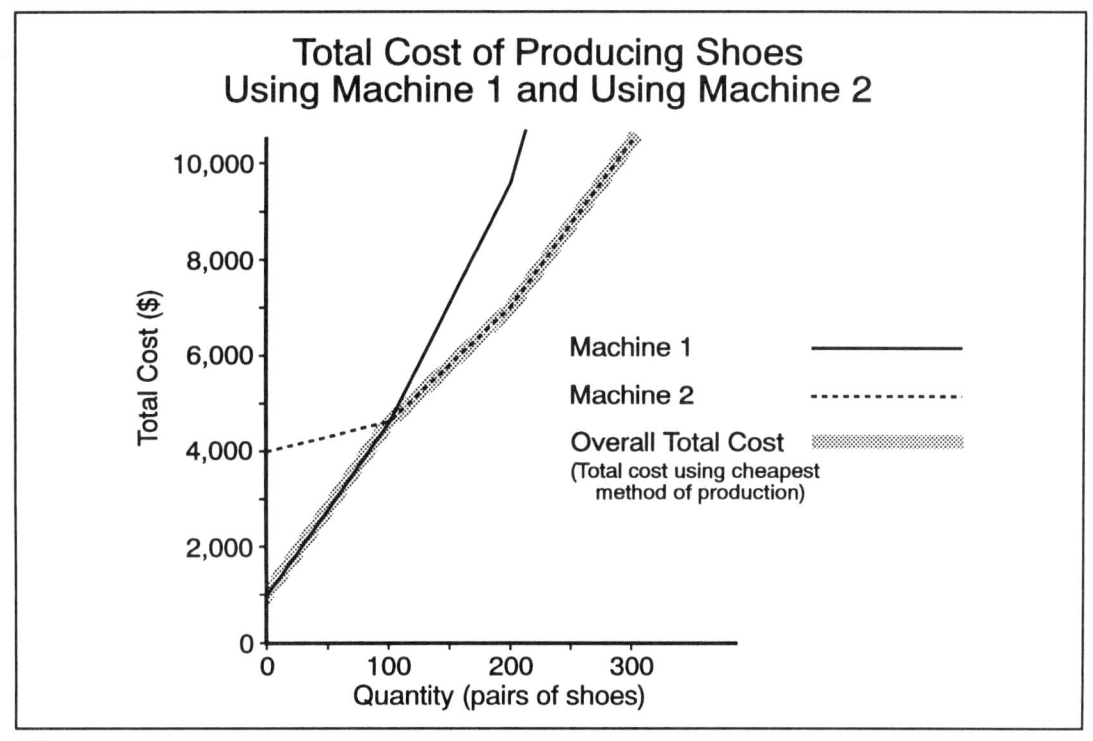

- Machine 1 ———
- Machine 2 - - - - - -
- Overall Total Cost ▓▓▓▓ (Total cost using cheapest method of production)

Figure 19

Marginal Cost and Marginal Revenue of Producing Shoes

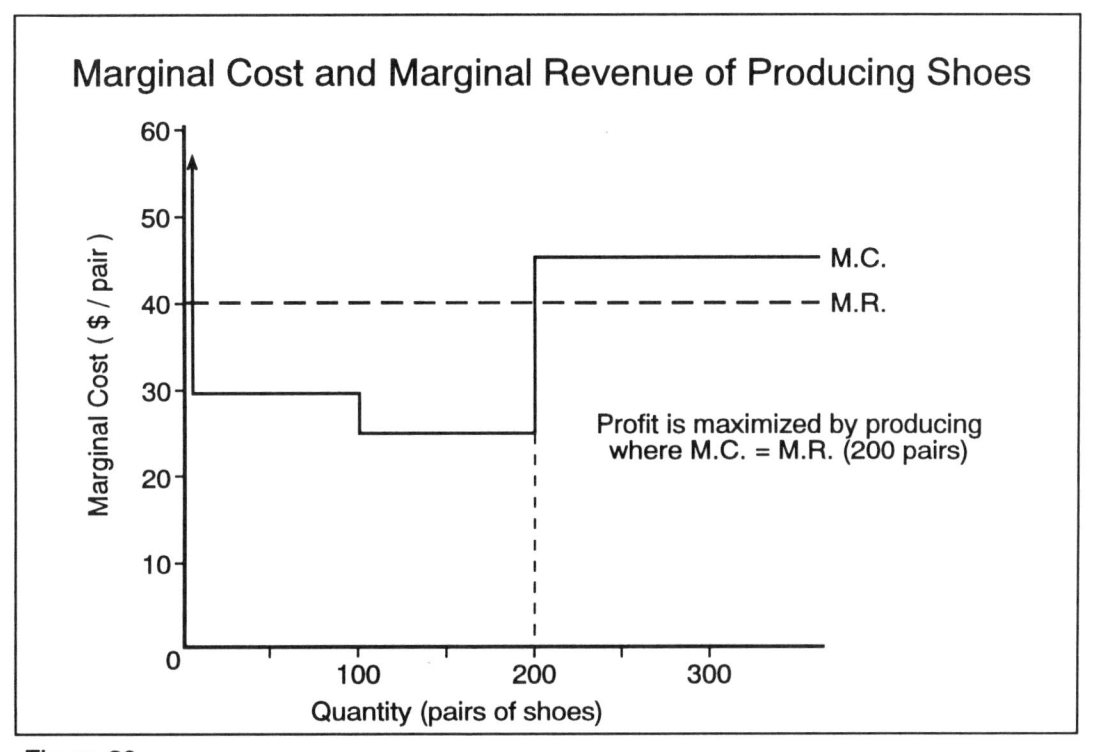

— M.C.
— — — M.R.

Profit is maximized by producing where M.C. = M.R. (200 pairs)

Figure 20

On the same graph, we can plot marginal revenue. The company can sell each additional pair of shoes it produces for $40, and it does not have to change its price when it produces more shoes. Hence, each additional pair brings in an additional $40 in revenue. That means marginal revenue is $40. From our graph in Figure 20, we see that marginal revenue crosses marginal cost at Q = 200. Therefore this is the number of shoes that maximizes the company's profits.

Before we leave this example, however, we should verify whether the company should go into business at all. It should do so only if its average cost is less than the price it can get for each unit it produces. The average cost at Q = 200 is $35.[9] This is $5 below the price of each pair of shoes, so the company will make a profit and should go into business.[10]

Suggested Additional Reading

Edwin Mansfield, MICROECONOMICS: THEORY AND APPLICATIONS 179-258 (8th ed. 1994).

Robin Marris & Dennis C. Mueller, *The Corporation, Competition and the Invisible Hand*, 18 J. ECON. LIT. 32 (1980).

George J. Stigler, THE THEORY OF PRICE 104-114 (3d ed. 1966).

---

[9] Total cost is $7000 — $4000 for machine 2, $500 for producing the first 100 pairs of shoes, and $2500 for producing the next 100 pairs of shoes.

[10] The maximum total profit the company can earn is [P - A.C.]·Q = $1000. Hence if each machine had cost an additional $1000 or more, it would not have paid for the company to go into the shoe business at all.

3
Market Dynamics and Equilibrium

A. Purely Competitive Markets

The first market structure at which we will look is that of the purely competitive market. Competitive markets generally are characterized by a large number of producers each producing the same good. In such a market, a consumer who has purchased a good from one producer can go to another for the good if the consumer becomes dissatisfied with the original producer, as might occur, for example, if the original producer decided to raise its price. The consumer's ability to switch producers greatly constrains how a producer will go about pricing its product to maximize its profit.

To best understand competitive markets, it is helpful to set out the formal definition of such a market. A purely competitive market is characterized by four attributes:

(i) The product sold by any producer in the market is identical to that sold by any other producer. Thus, the goods produced by each manufacturer are perfect substitutes for one another;

(ii) No buyer or seller in the market is so big that its decision about how much of the good to buy or sell will affect the market price. In other words, both consumers and producers act as price takers;

(iii) All resources in society (i.e. productive inputs) are perfectly mobile. Resources can be redeployed from production of one good to another, or from one firm to another. Also, consumers can change from purchasing the goods of one producer to purchasing the goods of another. This does not mean that such redeployment can be done immediately and without cost, so there is still a short run during which redeployment of some inputs will not occur;

(iv) Consumers and producers all have perfect knowledge. This means that consumers know the price charged by each producer. Providers of inputs (laborers and owners of capital) know how much each producer will pay for the resources they provide. Producers know the technology used by their competitors.

Obviously, the perfectly competitive market is a simplified theoretical construct that never exists in the real world. Nonetheless, studying such markets provides insights into how producers and consumers in markets that are competitive, albeit imperfectly so, might behave.

In our example involving the manufacturer of shoes, we have already seen how a producer who is a profit maximizing "price taker" will determine how much of the good to produce. For a price taker, because production and sale of an additional unit of a good does not change the price at which the producer can sell the other units it produces, such production and sale allows the producer to obtain additional revenues equal to the price of that unit. In other words, for a firm in a competitive market, marginal revenue equals price. A producer whose marginal revenue equals price (P) will choose to produce more and more of a good until the marginal cost

36 MICROECONOMIC PREDICATES TO LAW AND ECONOMICS

of the last unit equals the price.[11] Until this point is reached, marginal cost is less than price and the producer can increase profits by (P - M.C.) if it produces an additional unit. After this point, marginal cost exceeds price and the producer losses profits of (M.C. - P) by selling an additional unit.

Another way of thinking about such producers is to note that each one will face a demand curve represented by a horizontal line at the market price. If the producer prices its good above P, it will not be able to sell any units of the good because consumers will buy the good for P elsewhere. If the producer priced the good at some value less than P, it would not be profit maximizing because it could increase its price to P, sell the same number of units, and make more money per unit. Hence the producer will price its good at P and maximize profit by producing up to the quantity where marginal cost rises to that price.

1. *Competitive markets in the short run*

In a competitive market in the short run, we can define an industry supply curve, which along with the industry demand curve that we derived from consumer choice theory would allow us to analyze the market in terms of supply and demand. At any given price, the industry supply curve is the sum of the quantities that each producer would be willing to provide at this price. But we have already seen that an individual producer will be willing to produce more and more units until its marginal cost rises to P. Thus, the quantity that each firm is willing to supply when the market price is P is given by that firm's marginal cost curve at price P. The industry supply curve, then, is just the horizontal sum of all the producers' marginal cost curves. In the short run, in a competitive market, firms operate at a point where marginal cost is increasing, hence the horizontal sum is increasing as well. In other words, the short run supply curve is a curve with positive slope.

Now that we know what the supply and demand curves represent in a competitive market, we can see how the law of supply and demand determines the price for a good and the total quantity of the good produced by the entire industry. We know that at any price P, the amount of the good consumers purchase will be the quantity that is demanded at that price (i.e. the state of the market is represented by the point (P,Q_D) on the demand curve). Similarly, at price P, the amount produced will be the quantity corresponding to P on the supply curve (i.e. the state of the market is represented by the point (P,Q_S) on the supply curve). In equilibrium, however, every unit produced is sold to consumers, and every unit demanded by consumers is produced and sold by producers. Hence, Q_D equals Q_S, and the equilibrium price and quantity of the good is represented by the intersection of the supply and demand curves.[12] This is illustrated in Figure 21.

---

[11] This is illustrated by the graph labelled "The Relationship of Profit to Average and Marginal Cost," in Figure 18, above. This assumes, of course, that the producer cannot avoid losing money by not producing at all. In the short run, the producer will not produce any units of the good if its variable average cost exceeds price.

[12] Equilibrium is defined as a state of the economic system where rational choice by consumers and profit maximization by producers would not cause the price, quantity demanded or quantity supplied to change.

Equilibrium in a Competitive Market

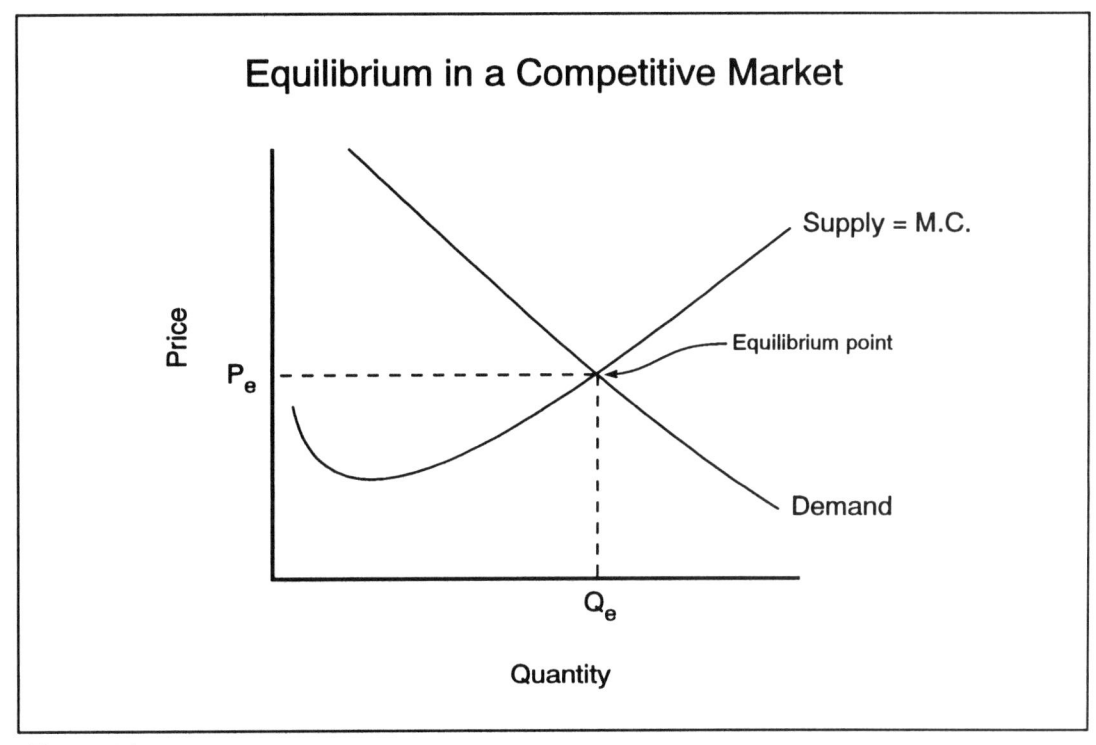

[Figure: Graph showing Supply = M.C. curve intersecting Demand curve at Equilibrium point (P_e, Q_e). Axes labeled Price (vertical) and Quantity (horizontal).]

Figure 21

To see why, consider what would happen if Q_D were greater than Q_S. In that case, there would be a shortage of the good in the market. Some individuals who would be willing to pay more than the market price would not be able to buy the good. Producers could raise their price, say by ΔP, and still sell all the units of the good that they produce. As profit maximizers they would do so, which would mean both that producers would be willing to produce more of the good **and** that some consumers who demanded the good at Price P would not want it at Price P+ΔP. In other words, at this price the quantity supplied would increase and the quantity demanded would decrease, reducing the shortage of the good. This increase in price would continue until the rise in supply and drop in demand caused Q_D to equal Q_S. By a similar argument, if Q_D were less than Q_S, then there would be an excess of the goods on the market, and some producers would have unsold goods. These producers could increase their profits by lowering their price and selling more units of the good. This would continue until the demand increased and the supply decreased just to the point at which Q_D equalled Q_S. Thus, as asserted, the market would not be in equilibrium unless Q_D equals Q_S.

2. *Competitive markets in the long run*

Producers face additional competitive constraints in the long run. In the short run, even with firms producing at quantities such that price equals marginal cost, firms can earn a positive economic profit (*i.e.* a greater than normal return on their investment). They can do so because other firms not already in the market, seeking the same high return, cannot costlessly shift their

38 MICROECONOMIC PREDICATES TO LAW AND ECONOMICS

resources to produce the good. Because new firms will see a cost to enter the market that existing firms do not see, new firms will not enter the market in the short run just because existing firms are earning a super-normal profit. Thus the price of the good can remain high enough to provide firms already in the market with a positive economic profit.

In long run equilibrium, however, firms in a competitive market cannot earn a positive economic profit because there are no barriers to new producers entering the market or to existing firms increasing or decreasing production. In the long run, existing firms have to build new plants and re-equip themselves. Hence, they see no cost advantage over new firms for this longer time horizon. If the industry were earning positive economic profits, then, in the long run, firms would invest in plants and equipment, increasing production in the industry, because they could earn a greater than normal return by doing so. Firms would continue to enter the market and otherwise increase production, causing the price to fall until the economic profits of firms in the industry fell precisely to zero. At this point, there is no longer an incentive for firms to enter the industry or increase production. If the industry were earning negative profits, then, in the long run, firms would invest in alternative endeavors, exiting the industry or scaling back plants and equipment until price increased just enough so that the firms earned zero economic profit. The key point is that in long run equilibrium, firms in a perfectly competitive market earn exactly zero economic profit. This is equivalent to firms operating at the point where price equals long run average cost. The state of a competitive market at long run equilibrium is represented in Figure 22.

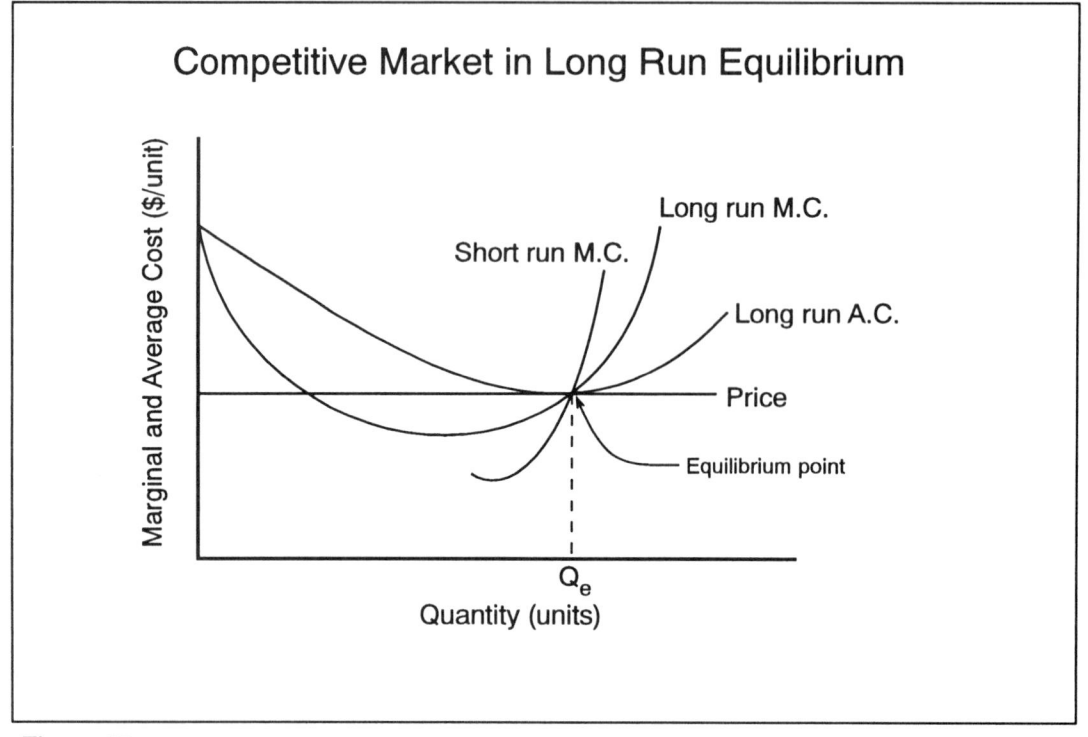

Figure 22

B. *Monopoly Markets*

Firms in monopoly markets operate very differently from those in competitive markets. A monopoly market is one in which the entire market demand is satisfied by one firm and no other firm threatens to enter the market. Therefore, the monopoly firm will affect the price by its decision about how much of the good to produce. It will be able to sell the good so long as there is sufficient industry demand at the price it sets. Just as a competitive market can be thought of as one in which individual producers see a flat demand curve at the market price, a monopoly market can be viewed as one for which the firm's demand curve is the industry demand curve, which by our derivation from the theory of consumer choice, slopes down as quantity increases.

We still posit that a monopoly, like any other producer, attempts to maximize its profits. The profit on the production and sale of any unit of a good is the additional revenue the firm derives from production and sale of the unit minus the additional cost of such production and sale—that is, marginal revenue minus marginal cost. For the competitive firm, the price was given and fixed, so production and sale of an additional unit brought in additional revenue equal to the price. For a monopoly, however, increasing the number of units produced and sold will decrease the price at which all units can be sold, because the demand curve slopes down as quantity increases.

One can derive a monopoly's marginal revenue curve from the industry demand curve. To calculate the marginal revenue at quantity Q, we must start by determining the monopoly's maximum revenue at quantity Q-1. To do so, we first use the demand curve to determine what price the monopoly can charge and still sell all Q-1 units of the good it produces. We then multiply this price by the quantity sold, Q-1, to get the revenue at Q-1. We can repeat this process for the quantity Q. The difference in total revenue that the monopoly can realize by producing Q units and by producing Q-1 units is the marginal revenue realized by producing the Qth unit (or more simply, the marginal revenue at Q). The following table illustrates the relationship between the demand and marginal revenue that a monopoly can realize for a simple demand curve.

THE RELATIONSHIP OF A MONOPOLY'S MARGINAL REVENUE AND DEMAND

Quantity	Price	Revenue	Marginal Revenue
1	$20	$20	$20
2	16	32	12
3	14	42	10
4	12	48	6
5	10	50	2
6	9	54	4
7	8	56	2
8	7	56	0
9	6	54	-2
10	5	50	-4

Generally, the marginal revenue curve will be a more rapidly decreasing curve than the demand curve, and when the demand curve is a straight line with slope -m, the marginal cost curve is a straight line with slope of -2m.

The monopoly will increase the quantity it produces until producing an additional unit generates marginal revenue that falls below marginal cost, or on a graph, at the point at which the marginal revenue and marginal cost curves cross. Suppose that the monopoly with the demand function shown in the above table had a marginal cost of production of $5 at every quantity of the good it produced. It would then produce 4 units of the good, which it will price at $12. Its revenue will be $48 and its total profit will be $28. The point of production for this monopolist, along with the economic profit earned by the monopolist, is shown in Figure 23.

1. *A comparison of social wealth under monopoly and competition*

Probably you have heard that competitive markets are good and monopolies bad. To understand why, we must introduce the concept of social wealth. Social wealth is the total dollar value of benefit society receives from a transaction, regardless of how that benefit is distributed. The social wealth attributable to a transaction is the sum of consumer surplus and producer profit from the transaction. When a producer sells a unit of a good to a consumer, the social wealth created is the value the consumer places on that unit minus the cost of producing that particular unit. But we have already seen that the demand curve represents the value consumers put on a particular unit of the good. Hence total social wealth created by production and sale of any total quantity of a good is merely the area between the demand and marginal cost curves.

Social wealth is maximized if firms continue to produce goods until the demand curve is no longer greater than the marginal cost curve.

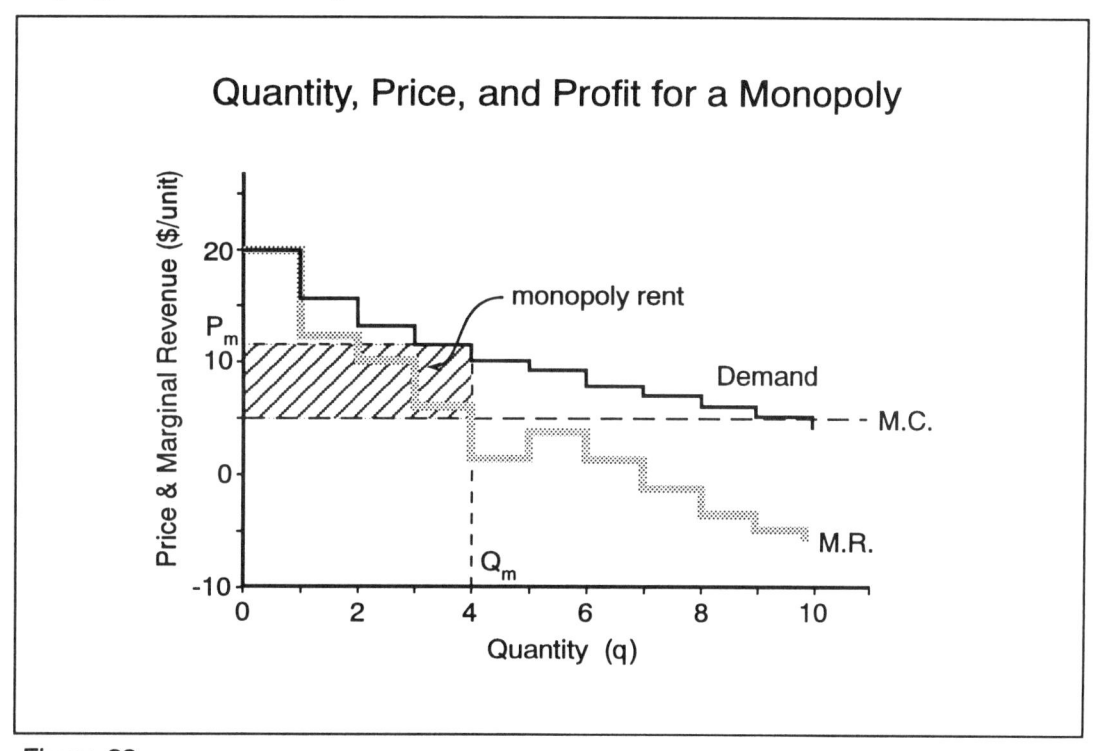

Quantity, Price, and Profit for a Monopoly

Figure 23

Recall, however, that in a competitive market, the marginal cost curve is the supply curve. Thus, social wealth is maximized if the industry produces just enough of a good that supply equals demand. This is precisely what we predicted would occur in a perfectly competitive market. In a monopoly, however, the producer stops when **marginal revenue** equals marginal cost. In other words, to avoid having to lower its price on units it could sell above marginal cost, the producer stops production before marginal cost rises to a level above demand, and this creates a dead-weight loss to society. Recall also that in a competitive market in long run equilibrium, economic profits are zero. Thus consumers capture all the social wealth from sales in such a market. In a monopoly market, however, the producer earns a positive economic profit. Restricting output allows the monopolist to capture some of that consumer surplus for himself. The profit that a monopoly earns by restricting output and charging a price above marginal cost is called a "monopoly rent." The relative creation and the distribution of social wealth between producer and consumer in competitive and monopoly markets is shown in the Figure 24.

Social Wealth Generated by Monopoly and Competitive Markets

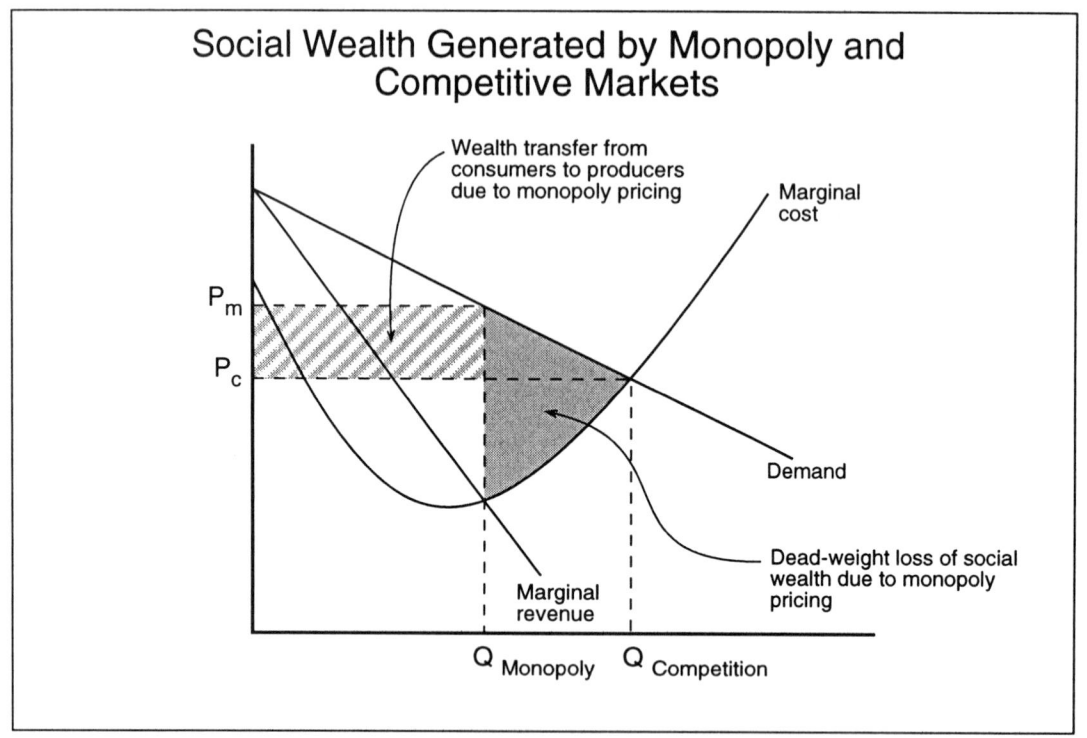

[Figure 24: Graph showing Pm and Pc price levels, Marginal cost curve, Demand curve, Marginal revenue curve, Q Monopoly and Q Competition quantities. Hatched rectangle labeled "Wealth transfer from consumers to producers due to monopoly pricing." Shaded triangle labeled "Dead-weight loss of social wealth due to monopoly pricing."]

Figure 24

Having discussed the relative benefits to society of competitive and monopoly markets, one caveat is in order. The analysis above assumes that costs are stable and do not change over time. The least cost way of producing a good today is the least cost way of producing it tomorrow. But, we know that in the real world technology changes and that this reduces the costs of production of existing goods and creates new goods that make our lives better off. Because the analysis above is static and cannot take into account changing technology, it is limited in what it can tell us about the relative benefits of monopoly and competition. Perhaps the discipline of the competitive marketplace provides great incentive for firms to be innovative. But perhaps, facing the prospect of profits only in the short run, firms in a competitive market will not invest as much as they otherwise would in new technology. Perhaps we need to give firms added incentive to innovate by allowing them to maintain a monopoly over the technological changes they invent. Economists and legal academics who study patent law debate this very point. Thus we see that despite the power of the economics we have developed thus far, it cannot definitively answer even relatively simple questions, such as whether monopoly is good or bad for society. It can only suggest benefits and detriments and leave the question for government policy-makers to ponder.

2. *Price discriminating monopolies and social wealth*

Despite the analysis above, it is not true that even under static economic conditions monopolies *necessarily* create less social wealth than competitive markets. Suppose that the monopoly facing the demand curve described by the previous table knew exactly how much each consumer valued each unit of the good. Because consumers have no alternative but to buy from the monopolist or do without, he can sell each unit to them at precisely the value they place on it. He will sell the first unit to the consumer who values it at $20 for $20; he will sell the second unit to the consumer who values it at $16 for $16; he will sell the third unit for $14; and so on. A monopolist who does this is called a perfect price discriminator. He will stop only when his profit from a sale is negative. But, because he is not repricing the first units when he lowers the price on subsequent units, his marginal revenue from production and sale is the price demanded. Hence he will continue to produce more units until demand falls below marginal cost—which is the precise criterion for maximizing social wealth. In the example that we used to discuss the relationship of demand to marginal revenue, the price discriminating monopolist will stop producing at either 9 or 10 units (he is indifferent between these because the marginal revenue from the 10th unit, $5, exactly equals the marginal cost of producing this unit.)

To sum up this discussion of price discrimination, the perfect price discriminator stops producing exactly at the socially optimal point, and he avoids imposing any dead-weight loss on society. Hence a perfect price discriminating monopolist will not cause a loss of social wealth. The problem posed by such a monopolist is one of how the wealth that flows from the sale of his goods is distributed. As the example above illustrates, the perfect price discriminator captures all the consumer surplus. His profit in the above example would be $57, and the consumers would get nothing out of the transactions. For this reason, society generally does not tolerate price discrimination by monopolies. In economic lingo, the problem with the perfect price discriminating monopoly is not one of efficiency, but rather one of fairness.

Perfect price discrimination, although theoretically interesting to economists, is of little practical significance in most market transactions. Not only are most markets not monopolies, but even if they were, it is difficult for a producer selling its product on a market to charge different customers different prices.

For economic analyses of certain legal doctrines, however, the possibility of perfect price discrimination is more realistic. Much of contract law addresses individuals engaging in face-to-face bargaining over particulars of an agreement. In a good number of contract cases, one party to the agreement is in a unique position to perform to the specification of the other party. Such situations may arise when the promisee seeks out the services of an especially talented individual; they may also arise in rescue cases where the rescuer was the only person who was in a position to help the victim. In such situations, not only might the bargain reflect a monopoly situation, it might also reflect a situation in which the promisor could assess the subjective value of the promise to the promisee, and could bargain for some (or even all) of that value.

One might be tempted to argue that contracts struck in such a monopoly situation should not be enforced because the deal struck might not be wealth maximizing. But the problem with monopolies is not that sales that are made are not wealth maximizing, but rather that the monopolist will refuse to make other sales that would increase wealth. Thus the real issue in contract cases involving a monopoly situation is not whether the deal struck was wealth maximizing, but rather whether the terms of the deal will discourage other wealth maximizing deals from being struck. In the context of face-to-face negotiations, the argument that enforcing a price struck in one deal will discourage others from contracting is more speculative than that a monopolist charging a high price in a market will discourage sales at any lower price. In fact, it may be that *failure to enforce such contracts* will discourage parties in monopoly positions from entering into other wealth maximizing contracts. In any case, the point of this aside about contract law is not to convince you one way or the other about how the law should deal with contracts made in a monopoly context, but rather to demonstrate that an understanding of monopolists' incentives, including the incentive to engage in price discrimination, is relevant to an evaluation of the doctrines of contract law.

C. Government Intervention into Markets

The microeconomic theory we have been studying not only allows us to compare the benefits of various market structures, it allows us to predict how the outcomes of market interactions (price and quantity) will change with changes in technology and consumer tastes. Just as significant for those, like us, who want to use economics to evaluate law, the theory allows us to predict how outcomes might change when the government intervenes in a market, such as when the government imposes a price ceiling or a tax.

To illustrate how the theory allows us to make such predictions, assume that the market for milk is competitive, and consider the supply and demand curve for milk shown in Figure 25. Suppose that a pharmaceutical company finds a way of manufacturing a bovine hormone that allows farmers to increase the milk production of dairy cows using the same amount of food, and without otherwise increasing the costs of tending to the cows. That new technology will lower the cost of milk production. Because the supply curve for milk is just the industry marginal cost curve, the costs of producing any quantity of milk will decrease and the new supply curve will fall below the original one. A new equilibrium will occur with a greater quantity of milk produced and consumed and a lower price for milk. This is illustrated in Figure 25(a). Consider the same initial supply and demand curves, only this time, instead of a new technological breakthrough, suppose a study shows that cows' milk is a major contributor to clogging of arteries, which causes heart attacks and strokes. Many people who otherwise would drink a significant quantity of milk decide to curtail their milk consumption. This means that at any given price the demand for milk will be less than that shown on the initial demand curve. The decrease in demand will lead to a new equilibrium represented by the intersection of the new, lower demand curve and the supply curve. At the new equilibrium, less milk will be produced and consumed and the price will be lower than the initial price. This is illustrated in Figure 25(b). We could just as easily predict the outcome for scenarios in which supply falls or demand increases.

Consider now the effect of a government tax on milk. Suppose the tax is 10 cents per gallon of milk and is imposed on milk producers. The effect of such a tax would be to increase the cost of milk production by 10 cents a gallon. The post-tax supply curve would be the original supply curve translated upward by 10 cents a gallon. This would decrease milk production and increase the cost of milk. In addition, we could illustrate the effect of such a tax on overall social wealth. Because the producers must turn over the tax to the government, the price they receive is 10 cents less than the market price. Their profit is the area between this hypothetical price line and their actual cost of production. Consumers pay the market price, so the consumer surplus is the area between the demand curve and the actual market price. Now however, there is another entity that receives wealth from the production and sale of milk—the government. It derives revenues equal to the 10 cent tax multiplied by the new quantity of milk

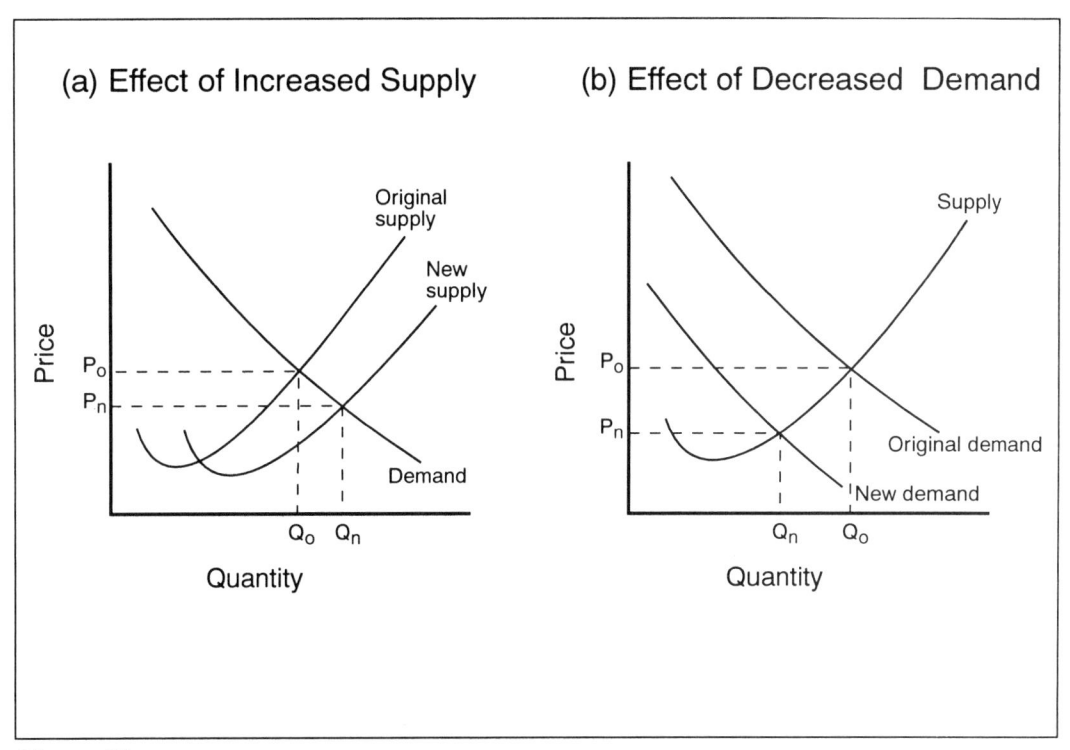

(a) Effect of Increased Supply

(b) Effect of Decreased Demand

Figure 25

produced. A graph of the social wealth after the tax is imposed illustrates each of these components of such wealth. The graph also shows that the tax results in a deadweight loss of wealth (similar to that caused by monopoly pricing) because those consumers who valued the milk higher than the cost of production, but not higher than the cost of production plus the tax, will no longer purchase milk. This is illustrated in Figure 26.

As a final exercise using our theory of market equilibrium, we can predict the effect of a price cap on milk. If the cap is above the market price for milk it will have no effect. If the cap is below the market price, then, at the capped price, producers will not be willing to produce enough milk to meet the market demand. There will be people willing to buy milk at the capped price who will not be able to buy it. This situation characterizes a shortage of the good. When there is a shortage, a significant amount of potential social wealth is forfeited. This is illustrated in Figure 27. In addition, consumers anxious to buy milk might be willing to bid up the price on an illegal black market. Since producers would be willing to produce more milk at this higher price to sell on such a market, price caps create a fertile ground for the establishment of such illegal markets.

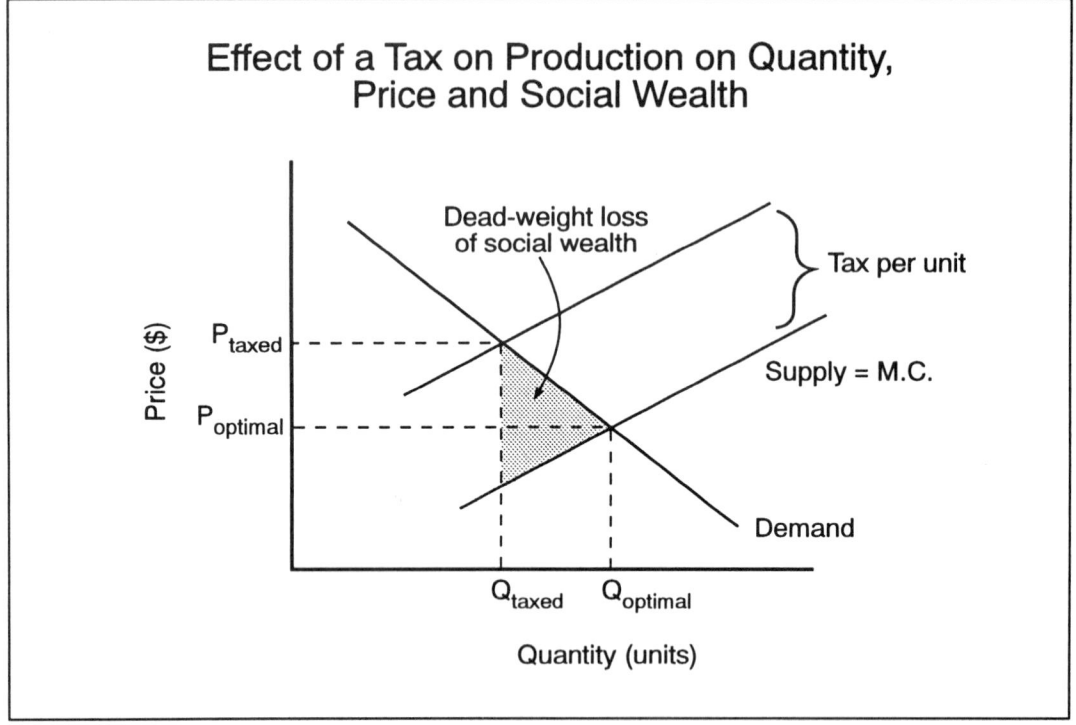

46 MICROECONOMIC PREDICATES TO LAW AND ECONOMICS

Figure 26: Effect of a Tax on Production on Quantity, Price and Social Wealth

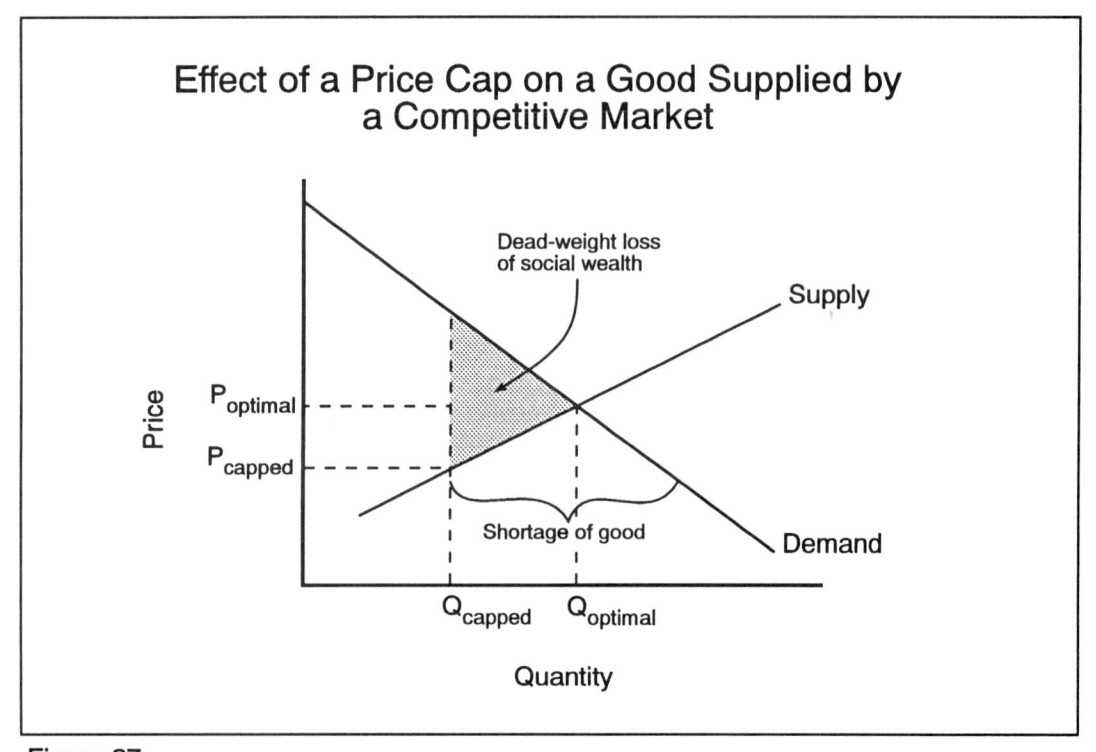

Figure 27: Effect of a Price Cap on a Good Supplied by a Competitive Market

The effect of a price cap on a monopoly market, however, might be very different than its effect on a competitive market. If the capped price was below the monopoly price but at or above the price at which supply equals demand, the result would be an increase in the supply of the good. This occurs because the monopolist's ability to maintain an artificially high price by restricting output is foiled by the price cap. If such a cap was costless to adopt and implement, it would also result in an increase in social wealth. The effect of a such a cap on a monopoly market is shown in Figure 28.

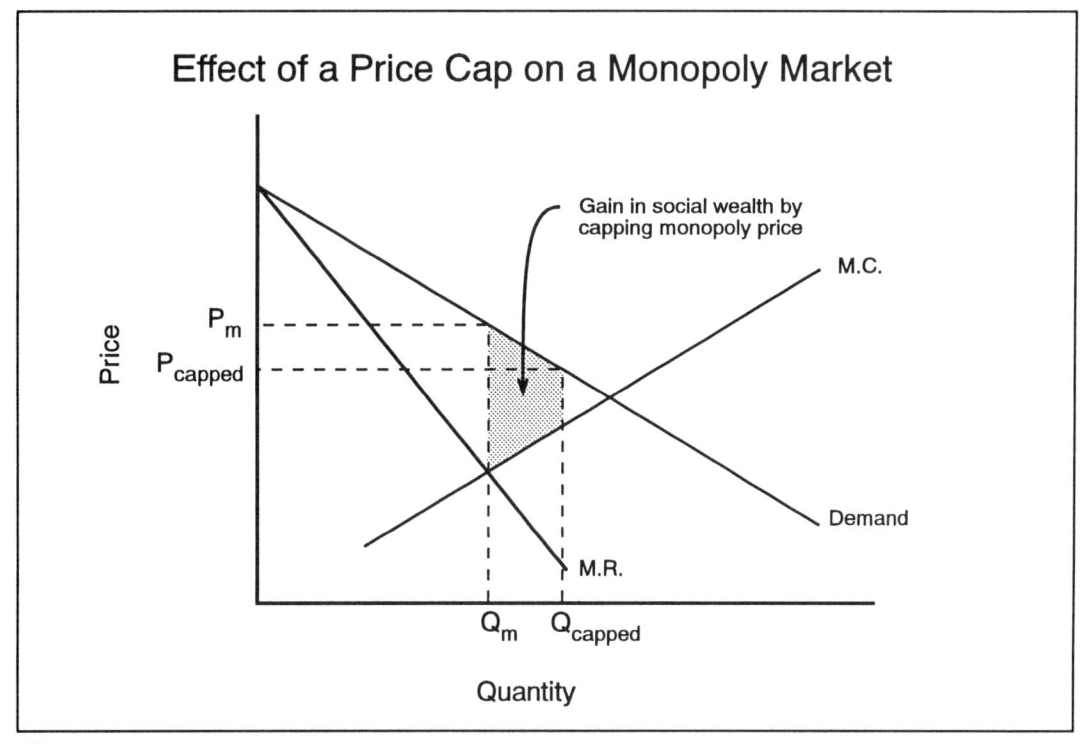

Figure 28

Despite the seeming benefits predicted for a price cap in a monopoly market, we must resist the temptation to draw the conclusion that such a cap is justified. First, adopting and implementing such a cap is costly, and we must consider whether the costs to the government of maintaining the cap exceed any benefits society might reap. In addition, there is a chance that the cap may fall below the price at which supply and demand intersect. If that is the case, the cap will decrease social wealth from the optimal level. We must balance the possible social cost of such an unwise cap against the benefit a price cap might bestow. Finally, we must remember that equilibrium theory says nothing about the incentives for changes in the underlying market. Imposing a price cap may discourage entry into the monopoly market by other producers attracted by the super-normal profits of the monopolist. The cap might result in a decreased incentive for others to improve technology and use their ability to produce at a lower cost to challenge the monopolist's position in the market. In the end the important point is not to decide whether a price cap in a monopoly market is good, but rather to use our economic theory to generate arguments about the wisdom of such a cap, recognizing all the while that our static economic model will never give a complete answer to that question.

Suggested Additional Reading

William J. Baumol, *Contestable Markets: An Uprising in the Theory of Industry Structure*, 72 AM. ECON. REV. 1 (March, 1982).

Herbert Hovenkamp, ECONOMICS AND FEDERAL ANTITRUST LAW 1-39 (1985).

Edwin Mansfield, MICROECONOMICS: THEORY AND APPLICATIONS 259-332 (8th ed. 1994).

F.M. Scherer, *The Welfare Economics of Competition and Monopoly*, in F.M. Scherer, INDUSTRIAL MARKET STRUCTURE AND ECONOMIC PERFORMANCE 8-38 (1970).

Joseph A. Schumpeter, CAPITALISM, SOCIALISM AND DEMOCRACY 87-106 (1942).

George J. Stigler, *Perfect Competition, Historically Contemplated* 65 J. POL. ECONOMY 1 (1957).

4
Efficiency & Social Welfare

Thus far we have considered how individuals order their preferences, how producers choose quantities to produce, and how markets, which aggregate the choices of individual decision-makers, provide mechanisms to enable producers to meet consumer desires. Implicit in our consideration of markets was the assumption that individuals are entitled to those goods which they voluntarily purchased in competition with other consumers who were seeking to buy the same goods. Sometimes, however, legal issues raise questions about whether this assumption is appropriate. Voluntary purchase requires wealth to compete for goods, and the outcome of such a system is highly dependent on the initial distribution of wealth in society. Law, however, often addresses concerns about fairness, which explicitly raises issues of wealth distribution. Even when legal issues do not raise concerns about fairness explicitly, they often address basic entitlements that determine individuals' wealth. We can't rely on individuals' abilities and willingness to pay for an entitlement when the assignment of that very entitlement significantly affects the goods for which individuals are willing and able to pay. Thus, one of the most significant areas of microeconomics for law and economics is "welfare economics," which addresses the normative measure by which society evaluates various policy alternatives. In other words, we must discuss what measure of economic "goodness" to use in order to evaluate whether a legal rule is economically justified, and as part of that measure we may want to consider how the rule distributes society's resources (*i.e.* wealth).

A. The Pareto Criterion for Efficiency

The first measure we will look at is that used by most microeconomists; it is called Pareto superiority. An economic change is considered a Pareto improvement (or equivalently the new outcome is considered Pareto superior to the old outcome) if it makes some individuals better off without making any person worse off. A state of the economic system is Pareto Optimal (or Pareto Efficient) if there is no Pareto superior state that society can reach. If we are using the Pareto criterion to evaluate our economic system, we say that a Pareto optimal state is "economically efficient."

1. *Distributional efficiency and the Edgeworth Box*

To illustrate how the Pareto criteria can be used to evaluate an economic outcome, we return to our two goods society, but this time we also specify that the society includes two individuals. Assume that the society can use its resources to produce a set amount of two goods, food and clothing, and that two consumers, Al and Barb, will use these goods. We can then construct a diagram, called an Edgeworth Box, to summarize the potential distributions of food and clothing between Al and Barb. To do so, we graph Al's indifference curves as we normally would. When the quantity of clothing Al consumes reaches that total produced by society he cannot obtain any more, so we can draw a line capping clothing at that quantity. Similarly, when the quantity of food reaches the total produced by society, that puts a right hand bound on the points

50   MICROECONOMICS PREDICATES TO LAW AND ECONOMICS

that Al can reach. By drawing these lines at the quantities of clothing and food produced by all of society, we form a box. Because any clothing and food not consumed by Al must be consumed by Barb, the distances from the point representing Al's consumption of each good to the lines representing the total quantities of each good in society represent the quantities of each good consumed by Barb. In other words, we can consider the box to represent Barb's utility, with the origin of Barb's indifference curves being the upper right-hand corner and Barb's utility increasing as the point representing the distribution of food and clothing moves down and to the left. This is illustrated in Figure 29.

Edgeworth Box of Al's and Barb's Preferences for Clothing and Food

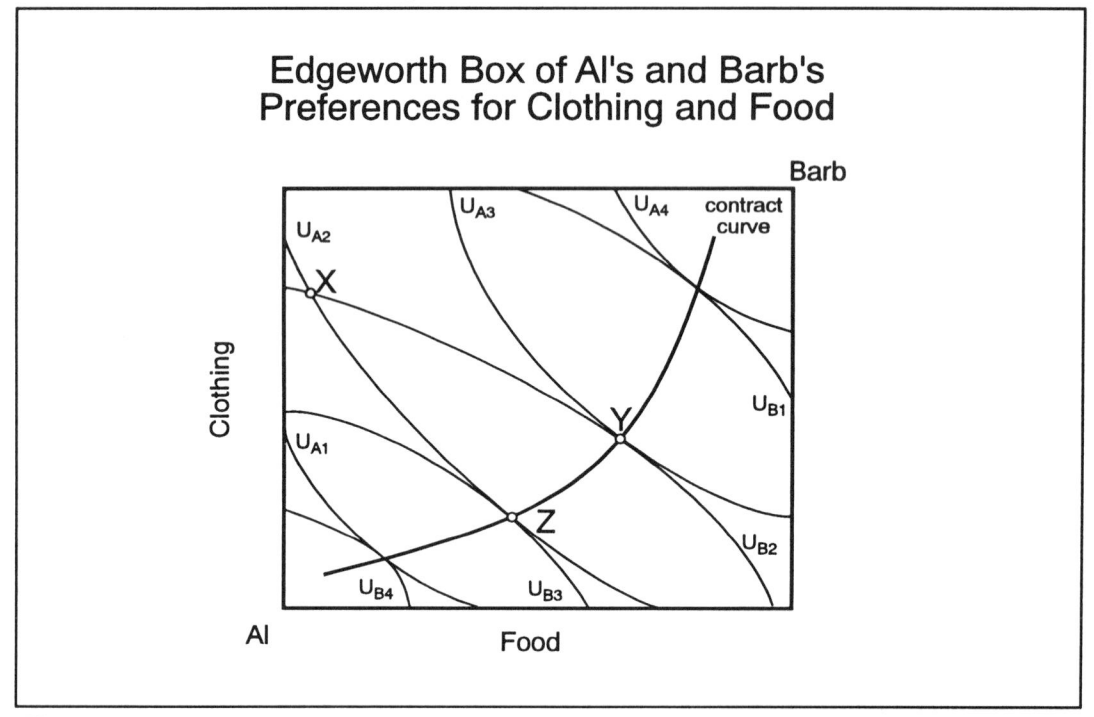

Figure 29

Suppose that initially Al and Barb started with the distribution of food and clothing represented by point X. This point is not Pareto Optimal because by trading food and clothing, Al and Barb can each make themselves better off. In particular, moving to any point within the lens shaped region formed by Al's and Barb's indifference curves through point X makes both individuals better off (and hence, in our two person society, no one worse off). Note that there was nothing unique about point X; for any point other than one at which Al's and Barb's indifference curves are tangent, the point lies on a set of indifference curves forming such a lens shaped region. Hence, Al and Barb will trade until they reach a point at which their indifference curves are tangent to one another. They will stop at such a point because at such a point it is not possible to increase one person's utility without decreasing the utility of the other.

The set of points of tangency of indifference curves is known as the contract curve. It represents all the points at which Al and Barb might stop trading because from each point on the curve there are no other points that Al and Barb can reach that make both of them better off. In other words, it represents the Pareto Optimal points for this society. We can translate the information from this Edgeworth Box onto another graph with Al's and Barb's utility as its horizontal and vertical axes. We can do so because every point in the box represents some level of utility for Al and some level of utility for Barb. On such a graph, the points on the contract curve map onto a boundary from which Al and Barb cannot both increase their utility. In other words, society cannot reach points to the right of and above this boundary. This boundary is known as the Pareto Frontier. If we identify point X on this graph with the initial distribution in our society, we can easily see which points on the boundary represent Y and Z on our Edgeworth Box, as these represent points on the Pareto frontier reached by respectively keeping Barb's and Al's utility constant. Al's and Barb's utility, and their relationship to points in our Edgeworth Box, are depicted in Figure 30.

Al's and Barb's Utility Possibility Curve or Pareto Frontier

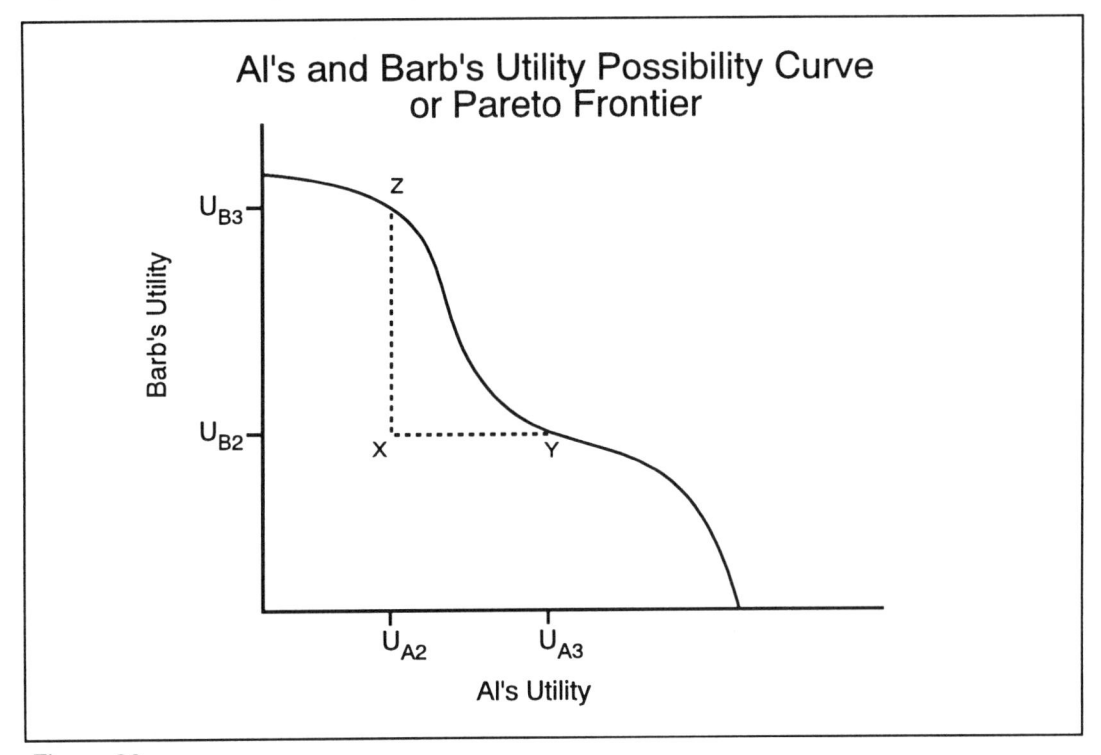

[Graph: Barb's Utility on vertical axis with U_{B3} and U_{B2} marked; Al's Utility on horizontal axis with U_{A2} and U_{A3} marked. Points Z, X, and Y are plotted, with Z on the frontier above, X interior, and Y on the frontier to the right.]

Figure 30

2. *Productive efficiency*

Thus far we have applied the Pareto criteria only to the question of distribution of goods among consumers in a society. We have looked only at distributional efficiency. We can, however, apply the same Edgeworth Box construct to the production sector. The axes would then be labelled by our production inputs, Capital and Labor, and each point in the Box would represent a level of resources devoted to the production of two goods, say clothing and food. Using isoquants for these two goods, we could then derive the curve representing efficient devotion of resources to produce these goods. We can generate a graph showing the tradeoff society would have to make if it desired to reduce production of clothing in order to increase production of food. The analog to the Pareto Frontier is called the "production possibility

52 MICROECONOMICS PREDICATES TO LAW AND ECONOMICS

curve." Points on this curve represent efficient use of resources to produce goods, or more simply, productive efficiency. The negative of the slope of this curve is the marginal rate of transformation of one product for the other. A production possibility curve for clothing and food, and its relation to the Edgeworth Box for these goods is illustrated in Figure 31.

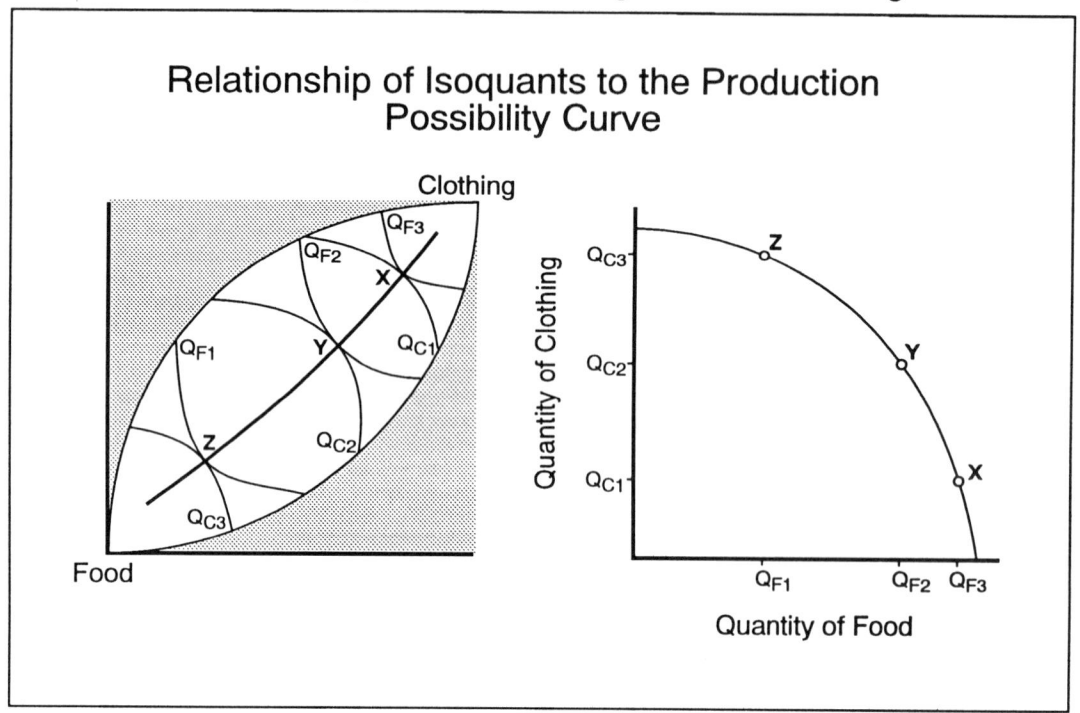

Figure 31

Generally the production possibility curve is concave to the origin, as shown. This reflects the logical premise that at some point it takes more resources to make an additional unit of a good after society has already devoted a lot of resources to producing a lot of that good, than it does for society to produce the first few units of the good. Put another way, making the first suit of clothing is relatively cheap. We can use workers with the best ability to sew, we can use the best machines and the best raw materials for fabric. After devoting the resources best suited to making clothing, it becomes more difficult to produce additional units of clothing; we have to resort to unskilled tailors and cheaper fabrics. When, however, production of one good directly interferes with the production of another—that is, when there are external costs of production—it is not always the case that the production possibility curve is concave.

3. *Allocative efficiency*

Our final use of the Pareto criteria will be to coordinate production and consumption. Suppose that producers are producing on the production possibility curve at a point where the slope of the curve is -2 (i.e. the marginal rate of product transformation of clothing for food is 2). But, suppose that consumers are at a point on the contract curve where the slope of their indifference curves is -1 (i.e. their marginal rate of substitution is 1). Although this society

EFFICIENCY & SOCIAL WELFARE 53

would exhibit productive and distributional efficiency, it would not be at a Pareto Optimal state.

To see why, note that either one of our consumers, let's use Al, could bargain with producers, agreeing to consume one less meal, if producers gave him two more suits of clothing. Producers could produce the two suits by reducing production of meals by one. Producers would be no worse off than they were before, but Al would be better off by one suit. Hence the point cannot be Pareto Optimal. Such a bargain can occur unless the slope of the consumers indifference curves equals the slope of the production possibility curve. When the two slopes are equal, the number of meals the producers would have to forego producing in order for them to produce an additional suit of clothing will have a value to the consumers precisely equal to that of the extra suit. Hence nothing is gained by switching from producing meals to producing clothing. An economy for which the mix of goods produced cannot be altered to make consumers better off is known as "allocatively efficient."

We can illustrate the criteria for allocative efficiency by placing the consumer Edgeworth Box inside the production possibility curve for a particular level of food and clothing production. Producers will move their operations along the production possibility curve, and simultaneously consumers will move along their now changed indifference curves until the slopes of the indifference curves and the production possibility curves are equal. The depiction of the allocatively efficient point using an Edgeworth Box and Production Possibility Curve is illustrated in Figure 32.

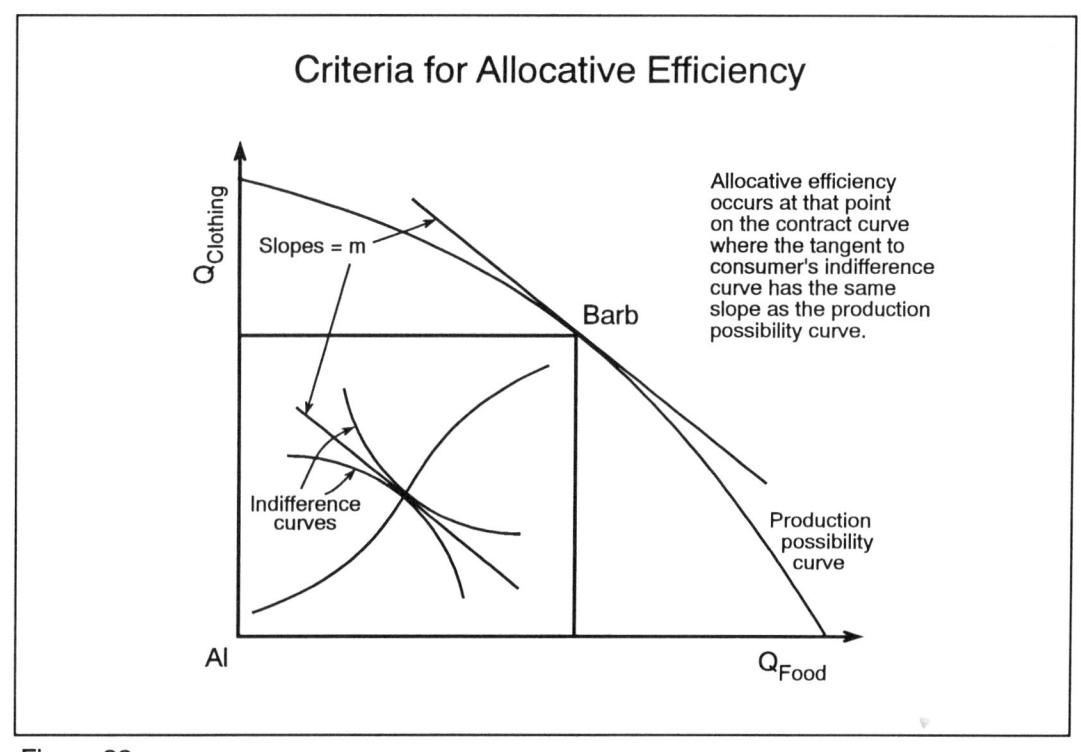

Figure 32

4. *Problems with the Pareto criteria for efficiency*

We can summarize our application of the Pareto criteria to the various sectors of society. Society will be in a Pareto Optimal (efficient state) only if:

(i) every consumer has the same marginal rate of substitution, or equivalently society exhibits efficient distribution of goods;

(ii) every producer has the same marginal rate of technical substitution of inputs, or equivalently society exhibits efficient production of goods; and

(iii) consumers' marginal rate of substitution equals producers' marginal rate of product transformation, or equivalently society exhibits allocative efficiency.

Economists are enamored of the Pareto measure of efficiency because it obviates any need for them to make inter-personal utility comparisons or for them to specify which consumers preferences win out over others. The Pareto measure is based on the notion of unanimity; an economic change is justified only if all participants in the economic system agree to it. It is also consistent with the ideas of consumer sovereignty and the voluntary nature of consumer transactions; if any individual enters into the transaction voluntarily it is assumed that the individual is made better off and therefore the transaction is good. But the Pareto criteria are not entirely uncontroversial.

The Pareto measure is biased towards the status quo. It does not justify many changes. The problem with the Pareto criteria is that it does not provide any means for comparison of many outcomes. For example, it does not justify any change between various points on the Pareto Frontier. More significantly, even off the Pareto Frontier, the Pareto criteria cannot be used to compare two economic states such that moving from either state to the other makes some people better off and others worse off. In a complex economic world, such as the one in which we live, that is a devastating limitation to the Pareto criterion: outside of a theoretical, simplified economic system, any real world change in policy or law is almost certain to make somebody worse off. Use of the Pareto criteria to evaluate changes in legal rules and governmental policy would allow any individual who might be made marginally worse off to block a change that might make millions of people better off.

Some social welfare theorists also criticize the Pareto measure of efficiency as unjust. The outcomes justified under the Pareto measure depend greatly on the initial distribution of wealth in society. Recall that starting at point X on our plot of Al's and Barb's utility greatly limited the set of points at which society might finally end up. The Pareto measure does not care whether the initial distribution of wealth or the final outcome distributes goods to members of society fairly or equally. In other words, although the Pareto criteria allow economic changes that make the poor better off, for the most part it justifies outcomes that mirror initial entitlements before bargaining or market transactions occur.

B. The Kaldor-Hicks Criteria for Efficiency and Wealth Maximization

Economists have come up with another, related measure of efficiency, called Kaldor-Hicks efficiency, which allows them to compare any two economic outcomes. An economic change is Kaldor-Hicks efficient if the new outcome makes those who benefit sufficiently well off that they would still end up with an increase in utility even if they compensated the losers enough to make the losers indifferent. For example, suppose that the policy change results in an increase in food and clothing consumption by Al of two meals and two suits. But the change causes Barb to lose two meals and one suit. Because Al could make up Barb's loss and still be one suit of clothing better off, this change would be Kaldor-Hicks efficient. It is imperative to note that the Kaldor-Hicks criterion does not require that Al actually compensate Barb. Hence the move is Kaldor-Hicks efficient even though it leaves Barb worse off.

So defined, however, the Kaldor-Hicks criterion is not a practicable means of evaluating economic changes. In our simplified example, it was easy to see that the overall increase in production by society was sufficient to allow Al to so compensate Barb. But often this is not the case. Suppose instead that the change allowed Al to get three extra suits of clothing, but cost Barb nine meals. Unless we know how much of a trade-off Barb requires in suits to make up for the nine lost meals, we cannot know if this change is Kaldor-Hicks efficient. A major problem with the Kaldor-Hicks criterion, in its abstract form, is that it requires a detailed knowledge of the preference functions (i.e. indifference curves) of every member of society.

For this reason, some economists, and the law and economics movement in particular, have posited a closely related measure of efficiency, called "wealth maximization." Wealth maximization replaces the trade-off of utility required by the Kaldor-Hicks measure with monetary value or wealth. Under the wealth maximization criterion, a change is efficient if it increases the wealth of winners more than it decreases the wealth of losers. Suppose in our example that suits cost $50 and meals cost $10. Then the change makes Al $150 dollars better off, and Barb only $90 worse off. Hence, under our wealth maximization approach, the change is efficient.

We can illustrate how wealth maximization provides a measure of the social welfare of any economic outcome by drawing curves representing equal social welfare under this measure on a graph with Al's and Barb's wealth as the horizontal and vertical axes. The curves represent points between which our two person society is indifferent. From the assumption that society cares only about wealth maximization, it follows that such societal indifference curves represent lines along which the sum of Al's wealth and Barb's wealth are constant, regardless of how the wealth is distributed between Al and Barb. In other words, this graph makes manifest that wealth maximization is concerned only about the total wealth of society, measured in dollars, and does not depend on how that wealth is distributed. Wealth maximization as a social welfare function is shown in Figure 33.

Wealth maximization is not a panacea to the problems of evaluation that otherwise plague the Kaldor-Hicks approach. It is still difficult to account for all the ways in which a change in a legal rule makes members of society better or worse off. Because changes in legal rules often cause the gain or loss of items for which no market may exist—things as diverse and hard to value as a clean environment, reputation, and self esteem—valuation problems posed by wealth maximization are not trivial. But at least they do not require that policy-makers know the preference function of every individual affected by a legal rule.

With respect to the criticism that notions of efficiency do not sufficiently take fairness into account, however, wealth maximization is more problematic than the Pareto measure. Wealth maximization takes as its measure of efficiency value determined by individuals' willingness and ability to pay. Hence, as does the Pareto measure of efficiency, wealth maximization

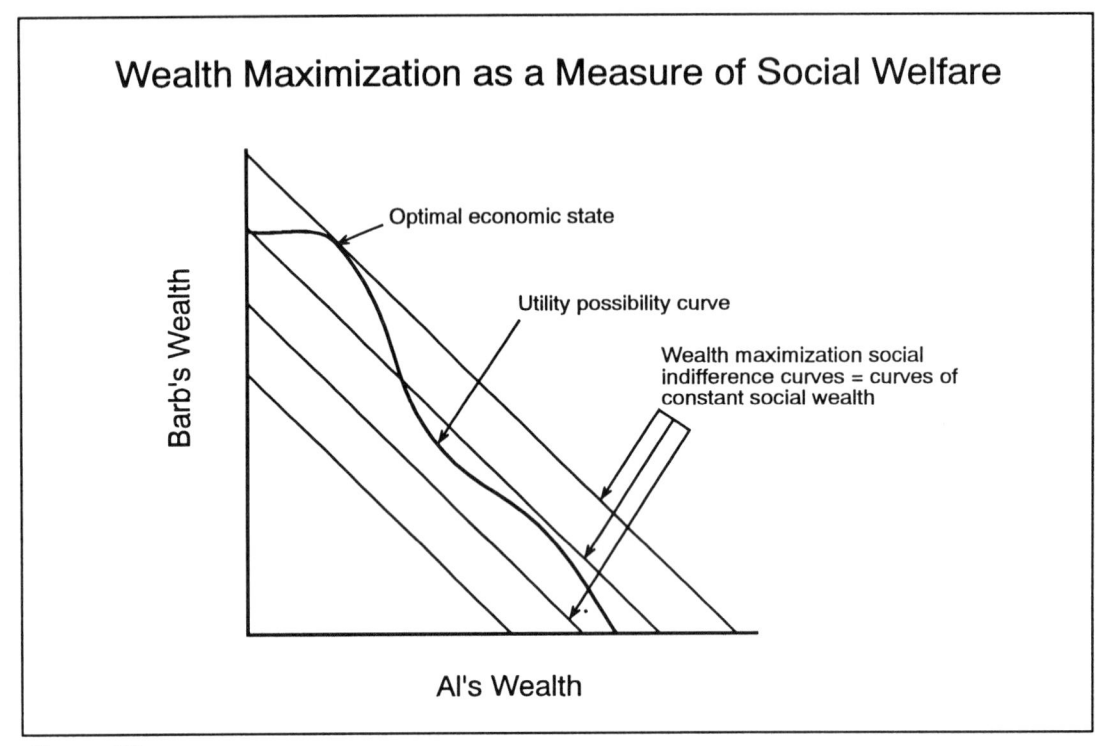

Figure 33: Wealth Maximization as a Measure of Social Welfare

(Graph with Barb's Wealth on y-axis and Al's Wealth on x-axis, showing: Optimal economic state, Utility possibility curve, and Wealth maximization social indifference curves = curves of constant social wealth.)

justifies outcomes that depend greatly on the initial distribution of wealth with which society starts. But, wealth maximization compounds the problem by allowing individuals with wealth to determine how legal entitlements are assigned, without these individuals ever having to pay for the entitlement. To put it another way, wealth maximization equates the value of a dollar to one person with the value of a dollar to another, regardless of whether the first person needs that dollar to buy food to keep from starving while the second person already has millions of dollars.

All of this suggests that one must be very cautious when using wealth maximization to evaluate potential changes in law or public policy. All else being equal, wealth maximization can indicate which of several potential legal rules is best. But, if the candidates for legal rules have significantly different impacts on the distribution of wealth in society, or correlate with the preferences of different classes of society, we will have to step back and ask whether the rule that is efficient is just, and whether it increases wealth at the expense of other social goals such as equality.

C. Other Social Welfare Functions and the Theory of Public Choice

1. *Equality as a social value and John Rawls maximin principle*

There are other social welfare functions that society could use to evaluate economic outcomes. For example, in "A Theory of Justice," John Rawls advocated his "maximin" principle, which prefers the social distribution of wealth that makes the least well off individual in society best off.[13] In other words, one outcome is preferable to another if the least well off individual under the first outcome has greater wealth than the least well off individual under the second outcome. Such a social welfare function places a great premium on equality because, given a fixed level of social wealth, social welfare under the Rawlsian measure is maximized by distributing that wealth equally to all members of society. Inequality in distribution of wealth, under Rawls's measure, is justified only if that inequality is a necessary consequence of a system that leads to sufficiently greater overall social wealth such that the least well off person in society is better off under that system despite the inequality in distribution. A social welfare function corresponding to Rawls maximin principle is illustrated by the graph in Figure 34.[14]

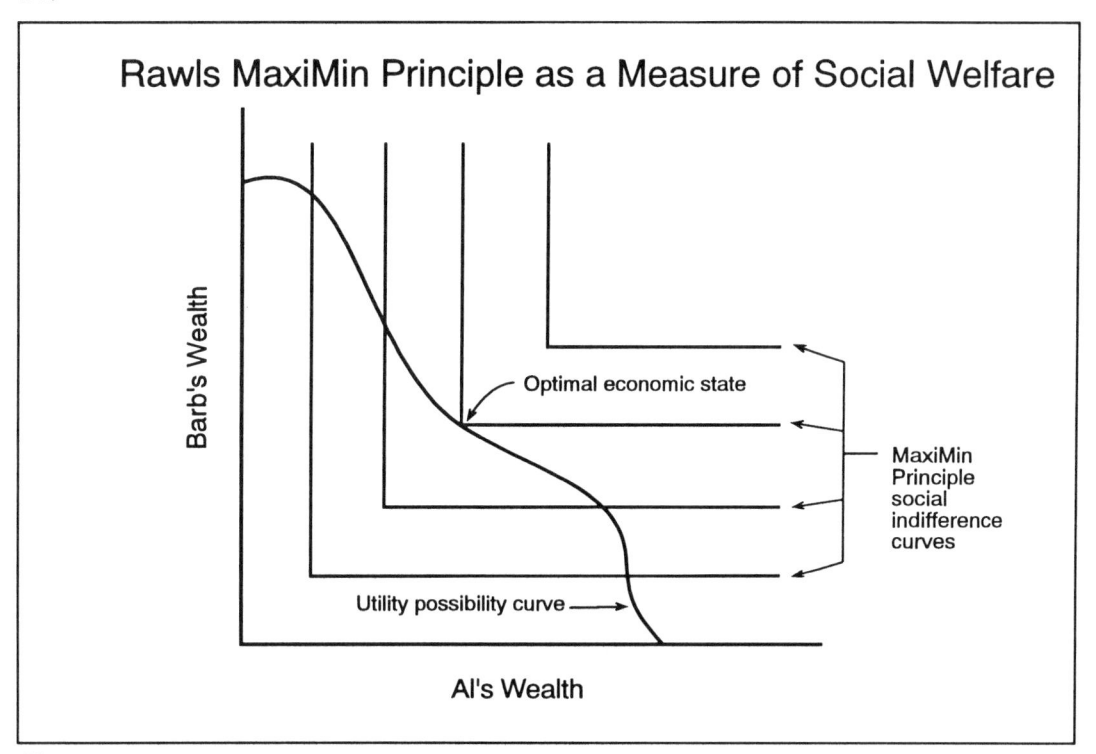

Figure 34

2. *Legislative determination of social welfare and public choice theory*

Given the problems inherent in any preset measure of economic goodness, and the value choices implicit in any choice between two economic outcomes, it seems logical that the choices

---

[13] JOHN RAWLS, A THEORY OF JUSTICE 75-83 (1971).

[14] Actually, the graph does not entirely capture the maximin principle. Under that principle, a change in economic outcome is good if it leaves the least well off person in society at the same level of wealth, and makes others in society better off. The graph depicts society as indifferent between such changes. But the graph is accurate to the extent that it depicts Rawls strong preference for equality as the most important measure of social welfare.

of policies and legal rules that lead to various outcomes might best be left to the political process. Essentially, this would allow politically accountable representatives to choose the social welfare function that will apply in any particular context. In a democracy such as ours, choices between maximizing wealth and various distributional concerns are the proper province of the legislature. Unfortunately, the economics of political decision-making, called public choice theory, provides reasons to doubt that the legislature can make these fundamental choices in a rational or even legitimate manner.

One problem with using legislative decisions to resolve these fundamental choices of social welfare stems from Kenneth Arrow's proof that it is impossible to structure a voting scheme that sensibly reflects the choices of voters and also determines preferences between all possible alternatives.[15] More specifically, no voting scheme can satisfy the following five conditions:

1. Transitivity—The preferences of the voting body (e.g. the legislature) must be transitive. That is, if the body would vote to prefer X to Y, and to prefer Y to Z, then it would vote to prefer X to Z.

2. Unanimity—The preferences of the voting body must reflect the unanimous preferences of its underlying members in that, if every member of the body prefers X to Y, then the body would vote to prefer X to Y.

3. Nondictatorship—The choices of the voting body are not dictated by anyone inside or outside the body (so no single member of the body can dictate outcomes).

4. Independence of Irrelevant Alternatives—The preference of the members of the body regarding two alternatives depends only on their feelings about those alternatives and does not depend on their preferences regarding other alternatives. This means that members of the body do not vote strategically and do not trade votes on various issues.

5. Unrestricted Domain—The voting process must provide an ordering of alternatives for every possible set of preferences of members of the body. Equivalently, the process must not declare impermissible any orderings of alternatives that a member of the voting body may hold.

Arrow's Theorem can be illustrated with a simple example: consider three legislators, denominated as A, B, and C, who are considering which of three programs, X, Y or Z, to fund. (Assume that each program will require all the dollars available to the legislature, so the legislature can fund only one of the three programs.) The following table summarizes the preferences of each legislator.

---

[15] Arrow first proved his theorem in 1951. KENNETH J. ARROW, SOCIAL CHOICE AND INDIVIDUAL VALUES (1951). A more accessible proof, attributed to William Vickrey, appears in DENNIS C. MUELLER, PUBLIC CHOICE II 385-87 (1989).

	LEGISLATOR	A	B	C
PREFERENCE				
1st Choice		X	Y	Z
2nd Choice		Y	Z	X
3rd Choice		Z	X	Y

Suppose that the legislators first vote on X versus Y. Because legislators A and C prefer X to Y, X wins. Then the legislators vote on X versus Z. Because legislators B and C prefer Z to X, Z wins. If, however, the legislators now decided to compare Z to Y, because A and B prefer Y to Z, Y would win. But this violates Arrow's first condition, for now the legislature has preferred Z to X, and X to Y, but prefers Y to Z.

Arrow's Theorem demonstrates that we cannot rely on perfectly rational political processes to resolve questions of social welfare (i.e. to resolve trade-offs between social wealth and other social goals). But we must be careful not to overstate the significance of Arrow's Theorem. For example, it turns out that there are certain classes of value-laden decisions for which a rational voting scheme will work.[16] In addition, we generally do not consider legislation to be illegitimate because it is the product of strategic voting, log-rolling or because choices were constrained by the congressional committee system, although all of these attributes violate Arrow's specifications for a sensible voting scheme.

There are, however, other problems with reliance on the legislative process. Assuming legislators respond to constituent pressure, public choice theorists have demonstrated that the political process is likely to be biased against the diffuse interests of the general public and in favor of the focused interests of smaller groups. This is so because there are costs to collective action.

To illustrate this phenomenon, suppose there is a possible change in the law that will cost 1,000,000 individuals $1 each. But the change will also benefit 100 people $5,000 each. In order for a legislator to know how the change will affect her constituents, each constituent must learn how the change affects them, and then communicate this by calling or writing their representative. For the 1,000,000 who are slightly affected, it is not worth their time and the cost of the phone call or stamp to inform their legislator. The 100 people greatly affected, however, have a great incentive to learn about the issue and to tell their representative how they feel. Thus, the information the representative receives would indicate that her constituents

---

[16] For example, a voting scheme can satisfy all five of Arrow's requirements if the underlying voter preferences are "single peaked." Essentially this occurs for any set of choices that can be ordered by a single variable. For instance, the level of government aid to the poor might be ordered on a scale of political conservatism: the less aid granted the more conservative the outcome, the more aid granted the more liberal the outcome. Because the issue can be so ordered, it is possible to devise a voting scheme for selecting the level of aid that satisfies Arrow's requirements.

would strongly prefer the change, even though the change causes a net loss to their overall wealth of $500,000. Because of the costs of collective action, the legislator gets the wrong signal and would vote the wrong way (assuming wealth maximization is the measure of how the legislator should vote).

From the perspective of a legislator trying to ensure re-election, however, voting for the change might be the smart thing to do, even if the legislator knows the value each of her constituents puts on the change. The 1,000,000 voters who are minimally affected by the change are not likely to vote against the legislator because of her position on this change. The change is not sufficiently important for them to take it into account in their voting. But for the 100 people greatly affected, this issue is of greater significance. By voting for the change, the legislator might secure these 100 votes without forfeiting the votes of other constituents. In this way, our system of representative democracy is biased towards focused interests.

Suggested Additional Reading

Jules L. Coleman, MARKETS, MORALS AND THE LAW (1988).

Ronald Dworkin, *Is Wealth a Value*, 9 J. LEGAL STUD. 191 (1980).

Daniel A. Farber & Philip P. Frickey, LAW AND PUBLIC CHOICE: A CRITICAL INTRODUCTION (1991).

Anthony Kronman, *Wealth Maximization as a Normative Principle*, 9 J. LEGAL. STUD. 227 (1980).

Edwin Mansfield, MICROECONOMICS: THEORY AND APPLICATIONS 489-542 (1994).

Mancur Olson, THE LOGIC OF COLLECTIVE ACTION: PUBLIC GOODS AND THE THEORY OF GROUPS (1965).

Richard A. Posner, *Utilitarianism, Economics and Legal Theory*, 8 J. LEGAL STUD. 103 (1979).

Symposium on Efficiency as a Legal Concern, 8 HOFSTRA L. REV. 485 (1980).

5
Market Imperfections

Thus far we have explored perfectly competitive markets and perfect monopolies. Economists are especially interested in competitive markets because if the market for all goods is perfectly competitive, then the economy will satisfy all of the conditions for Pareto Optimality. Unfortunately, most markets are not perfectly competitive; some market imperfections exist. The questions to which we now turn are: What are the effects of such market imperfections; and how might the government, by making or amending laws, best try to remedy those imperfections or otherwise alleviate their detrimental effects. Armed with the tools for evaluating economic outcomes—notions of efficiency—we are ready to discuss these questions.

A. Natural Monopolies

We have already considered one kind of market imperfection—the existence of monopoly power. Monopoly power can result from several phenomena: the firm may have superior technology, allowing it to supply all of the market demand at a price below that which other producers can match; the government may license monopoly power, as it does for utilities; or the producer may have a patent on a production process that legally sanctions it to prevent others from using the process. If monopolies are left free to maximize prices we have already seen that they will restrict output and raise prices. In terms of wealth maximization, they will not produce the correct mix of goods because they will stop production at a quantity where the value of the next unit to consumers exceeds the marginal cost of producing that unit. The law generally disfavors monopolies, making monopolization and agreements in restraint of trade illegal.

Although economic monopolies that are not government sanctioned have detrimental effects on society, such monopolies tend to be unstable. Prompted by the rents earned by monopolies, other firms will seek to produce the good. Agreements between firms to restrict output or not compete, which may ease some of this competitive pressure, are not only frequently illegal, they are difficult to enforce. Each firm usually will be able to increase profits greatly if it can cheat on the agreement.

There is one situation, called a natural monopoly, for which a monopoly may be the stable market structure. This occurs when an industry's marginal cost curve continues to decrease even past the point at which demand crosses the curve. An industry that depends on a physical network to deliver its good, such as the retail distribution of electrical power to small users (residences and small businesses) tends to have this type of marginal cost curve.

To see why, consider an electric company that provides power to all the homes but one in a neighborhood. To provide power to that home, the company need only extend its existing distribution lines a small distance. For a competitor to enter the market and supply that home with power, it would have to build a new line from the point where the company generates the electricity (or receives it from the transmission grid) to the home. The existing company is obviously the cheaper provider. Moreover, the more extensive the company's existing service, the cheaper it will be to extend that service to other customers, because the cost of providing service is cheaper when the probability is great that some nearby house already receives electricity. Hence, the greater the number of customers served, the cheaper it is to provide the next customer (*i.e.* the lower the marginal cost).

When the production of a good is characterized by a decreasing marginal cost curve, it is cheaper to produce an additional unit of the good than it was to produce the existing units. It follows from this that if there were two firms in the market, the larger firm could supply additional units of the good more cheaply than could the smaller firm, and in fact more cheaply than the smaller firm supplies its existing customers with the good. In such a market, the larger producer will be able to steal away the smaller producer's customers by undercutting the price of the smaller producer. Eventually the smaller producer will be forced out of the market and only one firm will remain. Once the single firm remains, it can restrict output and reap its monopoly rent. Other firms will not enter the market, for they know that if they do, the existing firm can lower its price and drive them out. Thus, in this situation, competitive pressures will not destabilize the monopoly.

Because of the nature of the marginal cost curve for a natural monopoly, it is not economically efficient to require more than one firm to supply the good. Thus, rather than break up such a monopoly, the government tends to license it (to prevent others from even threatening to enter the market, thereby causing disruptions) and to regulate the rates the licensed monopoly can charge. In this way, the state attempts to prevent the monopoly from raising prices by restricting output, as an unconstrained profit maximizing monopolist would do.

Rate regulation, however, is not free from controversy. First, even with perfect regulation, the price will not be the socially optimal price. We know that the socially optimal price is achieved by setting price equal to marginal cost. But, because marginal cost decreases over the entire region of demand, at the point where the marginal cost curve crosses the demand curve, average cost is greater than marginal cost. Thus, if the government were to set price equal to marginal cost, the firm would lose money. No firm would agree to go into business under those constraints. Hence the best that government regulators can do is set price equal to average cost, and live with the resulting inefficiency, which is less than would occur if the firm could charge the monopoly price. Figure 35 shows the price and output that is socially optimal, and those that would occur under unrestricted monopoly and rate regulation.

In addition to the inherent limitations of rate regulation, there are practical limitations as well. It is very difficult for regulators to determine the average cost of the natural monopoly. Therefore, ratemaking is a time consuming, expensive proposition. Also, rate setters have to rely on historical costs to determine average cost. The higher the firm's historic costs the higher its allowed rates. Hence there is no incentive for a regulated natural monopoly to minimize its costs and resulting rates often are higher than necessary.

A final objection to rate regulation hinges on the limits of our static economic model. We now know that rate regulation will be imperfect and expensive. Moreover, the government regulates rates because it seems to be the best option according to the static economic model of markets. But by regulating rates, the state may prevent competition that eventually would encourage the development of new technology that would destroy the natural monopoly. The effect of such technological change can be seen in today's telephone market: with the advent of satellite and microwave communications, long distance service is no longer a natural monopoly, and consumers can obtain cheaper long distance rates because of the competition in the market. Critics of rate regulation argue that competition would have come to the market much earlier had the government not granted AT&T an exclusive monopoly to provide such telephone service.

Price and Output for a Natural Monopoly

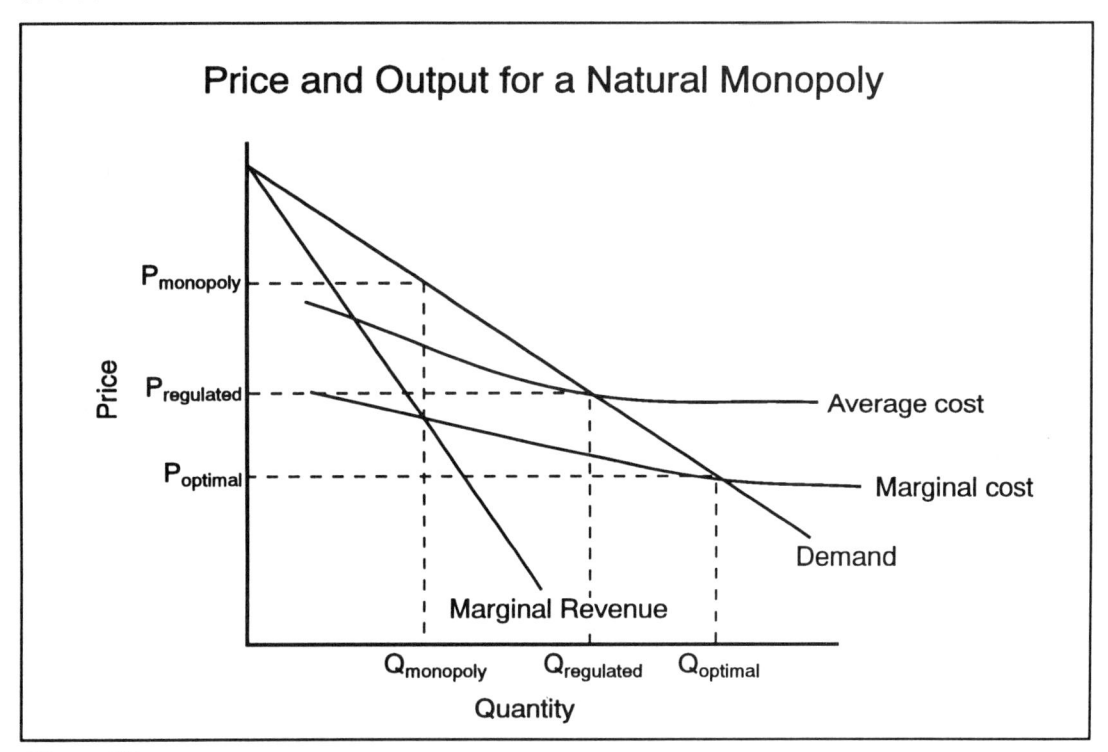

Figure 35

B. Externalities

Another type of market imperfection is known as an externality. Up until now we have assumed that the consumer who purchased a good got the full benefit of using it, and in using it did not impose costs on anyone else in society. Similarly, we assumed that the producer derived the full payment for the production and sale of the good, and bore the full cost of such production and sale. For many goods, however, consumption or production either bestows benefits on an individual or entity not party to the market transaction, or imposes costs on such "third persons." We can illustrate the effects of third party costs and benefits with two simple examples.

1. *External costs*

Suppose that Pollutco manufactures widgets in a plant located next to a residential neighborhood. Operation of the plant is noisy, and shipping of widgets causes traffic that the local neighbors dislike. The greater the number of widgets the plant produces, the greater and longer the hours of noise, the greater the traffic, etc. Each neighbor would be willing to pay a small amount to have the plant decrease its production. When we add up the amount each neighbor is willing to pay to get the plant to reduce production, it comes out to $2 per widget. The plant is then imposing a $2 per widget external cost on its neighbors because this is the value of the peace and quiet the neighbors forego due to production of each additional widget.

If the neighbors do nothing and the plant acts as a profit maximizer, it will produce widgets until its private marginal cost curve crosses its demand curve. But, we have seen that the real social cost of production is $2 per widget greater than the cost that Pollutco incurs. Thus, social wealth would be maximized by having Pollutco stop producing at the point where the social marginal cost curve equals the demand for widgets. The graph in Figure 36 illustrates that external costs of production cause the quantity produced to be greater than is socially optimal (*i.e.* wealth maximizing). Note that if Pollutco's plant is the only one in the competitive industry that creates such costs, the optimal price does not change. If, however, the whole industry imposes similar external costs then the price at which widgets sell will be too high by some amount less than or equal to $2.

The Effect of External Costs in a Competitive Industry

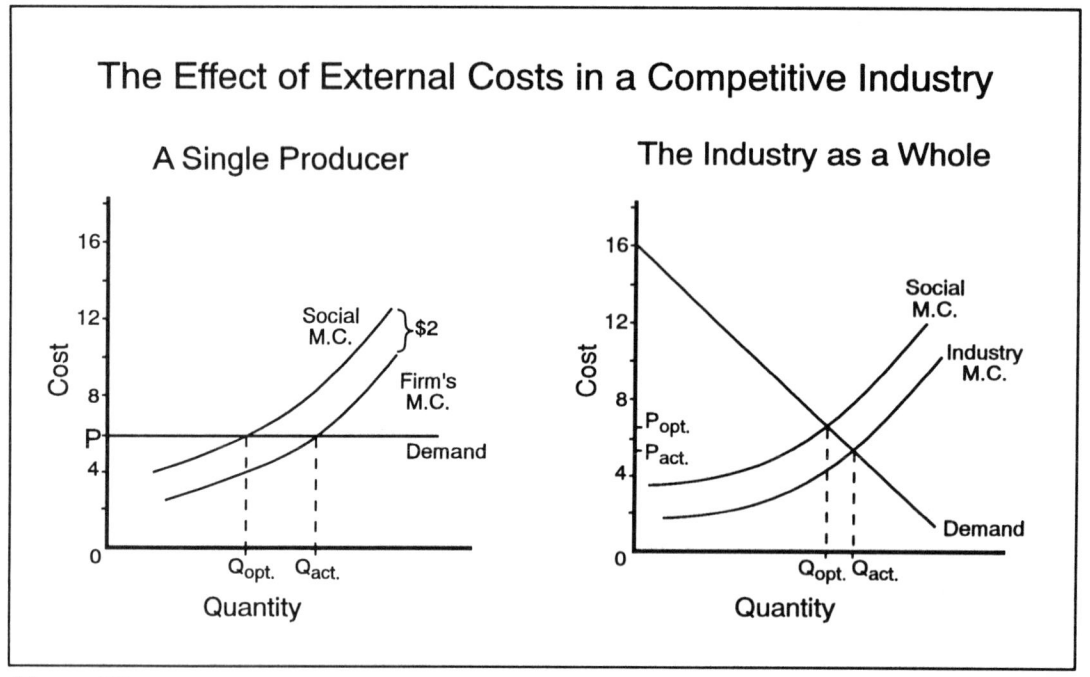

A Single Producer — Cost vs. Quantity, showing Social M.C., Firm's M.C. (separated by $2), Demand line at P, with $Q_{opt.}$ and $Q_{act.}$ marked.

The Industry as a Whole — Cost vs. Quantity, showing Social M.C., Industry M.C., Demand curve, with $P_{opt.}$, $P_{act.}$, $Q_{opt.}$ and $Q_{act.}$ marked.

Figure 36

There are several ways we might try to get Pollutco to produce the optimal quantity of widgets. We might limit their production to the optimal quantity. This, however, might be difficult to do, because it may be difficult to know the precise supply and demand curves facing Pollutco. Alternatively, we could impose a tax of $2 per widget on Pollutco, thereby making Pollutco "internalize" the external cost it imposes on society. This too might be problematic, because in the real world, measuring the magnitude of the marginal external cost is usually difficult. A third alternative would be to put Pollutco on notice that it is liable to its neighbors as a nuisance for any harm it might cause them. Then Pollutco can calculate the harm it causes, and factor that into its marginal cost. This is problematic also, because it might be costly to organize all the neighbors to get together to sue Pollutco.

2. *External benefits*

Now consider the Johnsons, who love to have a beautiful yard. The Johnson's demand curve shown in Figure 37 indicates the monetary value that the Johnsons place on their yard as a function of its beauty. As the yard gets more and more beautiful, they value the incremental additions of beauty at a lower and lower value. The beauty of their yard depends on how much time and money they spend on it. The marginal cost curve in Figure 37 portrays the beauty of the yard as a function of how much the Johnsons invest in it. We know that as rational economic actors, they would invest in their yard up to the point where the marginal value to them of more beauty equalled the marginal cost of making the yard that little bit more beautiful. We also know that if the Johnsons bear all of the costs and benefits of the yard's beauty, their investment in their yard would be efficient (i.e. wealth maximizing).

The beauty of the Johnson's yard, however, is appreciated by the entire neighborhood. Because of the nice view it provides from the neighbors homes, it increases the value of houses in the area. Figure 37 also reflects that the neighbors will have their own demand curve for beauty of the Johnson's yard. Then the social value of investment in the Johnson's yard is really given by a curve that, at any quantity, is the sum of the value of the Johnson's private demand curve and the demand curve of all the neighbors. Unlike with ordinary goods, the curves are summed vertically not horizontally, because appreciation of the yard's beauty by the Johnsons does not prevent appreciation of the beauty by the neighbors. The graph in Figure 37 indicates that the Johnson's will invest less than the socially optimal amount in their yard.

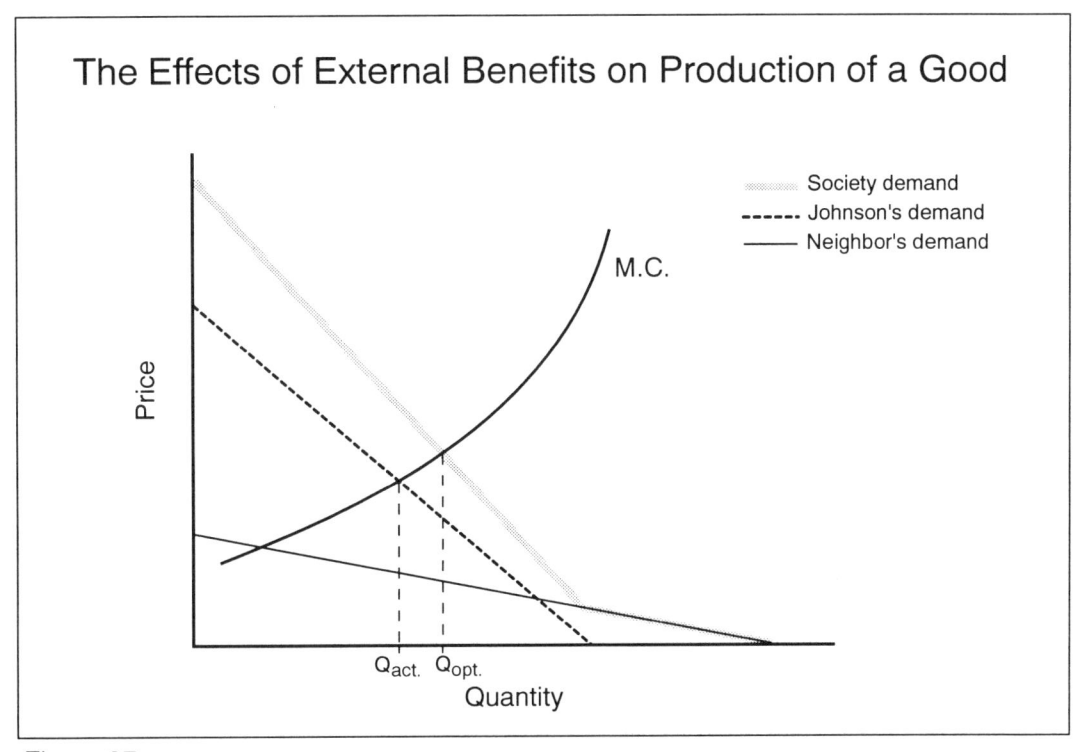

Figure 37

It is important to note that not every external benefit of production will result in an underinvestment in production. Unlike the case of external costs, the producer has an incentive to capture the value of the external benefit. The producer will not be able to do so, however, when: (i) consumption of the good by one individual does not preclude consumption by another (remember that appreciation of the beauty by one individual did not prevent the same appreciation by another individual), and (ii) the producer cannot restrict consumption of the good by those who do not pay for it (note that the Johnsons could not wall off the yard without destroying the benefit they bestow on the neighbors). Goods with these attributes are known as public goods. To show how an external benefit can be captured by a producer, suppose that the yard was so beautiful that individuals came from miles around to view it. In that case, the Johnsons could put up a wall around it, and charge admission for it. This is precisely what the owners of private gardens do.

To encourage greater production of the beauty of the Johnson's yard, the neighbors might try to subsidize the Johnson's investment in beauty. But coordinating such subsidies is difficult. It is necessary to determine how much each neighbor values the external benefit in order to determine how much each should contribute. Each neighbor will not want to reveal her full value because by doing so each can get the benefit of the subsidy by others without paying her fair share. In economic lingo, each has an incentive to "free ride" on the benefits provided by the others.

C. Imperfect Information

A third type of market imperfection is imperfect information. If consumers or producers do not have perfect information about products they might purchase, such as how food might taste or what machinery might do, they might not choose the product that best meets their needs. If consumers do not have perfect information about the price of goods, and producers about the price of inputs, they might purchase goods or inputs from an entity that charges more than others for the identical item. If producers do not have perfect information about the technology, costs and revenues of others in the market, they may incorrectly decide to enter the market or refrain from entry.

There are situations in which, at the time of a decision by a consumer or producer, certain information cannot be known. For example, if an investor buys corn futures in May, he cannot know what the weather will be like prior to the harvest in July and August. When information is unavailable at any price, we say it is incomplete, but not imperfect. Each individual will make decisions based on the best available information. When information could be obtained, but there is a significant cost to obtaining the information, we say that the information is imperfect. Producers and consumers may well decide to spend money to determine the information, and this will add to the cost of any transaction.

As the examples above illustrate, perfect information is crucial to all aspects of market dynamics and non-market transactions. Nevertheless, we should not overstate the impact of imperfect information on our analyses of whether an economic system is efficient. If the imperfections in information are minor, for instance if the consumer does not know that one producer charges 1¢ more per pound of filet mignon than others, they are not likely to create significant deviations from the otherwise efficient equilibrium.[17]

D. Transaction Costs

The final market imperfection that we will address is "transaction costs." As the label suggests, these are costs that arise by the very act of engaging in economic transactions. For example, in order to shop for groceries I must drive to the supermarket, using gasoline and taking up my time. If one supermarket is ¼ of a mile from my house, and the next one is 3 miles, I am apt to shop at the former store, even if the latter one has lower prices. Transaction costs are even more significant in non-market transactions. If an individual wants to enter into a contract, they will want a lawyer to check to ensure that it is enforceable, and perhaps to write the contract so it is clear and will be enforced according to the individual's understanding.

There are other types of transaction costs other than the direct costs of arriving at an agreement. Information costs can be viewed as a type of transaction cost. Implicit in the contracting example above was the fact that the individual did not have the requisite information to evaluate the enforceability of the contract. Thus, even when an individual can obtain the information needed to evaluate an economic choice (*i.e.* information is imperfect), the individual may have to pay to acquire the information. Such costs are called, not surprisingly, information costs. Many contracts involve promises for future performance. A party to such a contract may have to spend money to determine that the other party has complied with the terms of the contract. Such costs are called monitoring costs. Finally, an individual should consider what will happen if either she or the other party breaches the contract. In order to enforce the contract, a party must sue and get a court order, and then get the sheriff to enforce the order. This process too is costly. Such costs are called enforcement costs. All of these different costs—negotiating costs, information costs, monitoring costs and enforcement costs—can cause the actual outcome of transactions to deviate from the efficient ideal.

---

[17] At this point some economists are bound to jump up and complain. Once one deviates from perfect competition, it is impossible to prove how far this will lead the entire economy to wander from the efficient outcome guaranteed by competition. In fact, as long as the entire economic system is not perfectly competitive, the "theory of the second best" states that it is not necessarily true that reducing deviations from competition will result in an outcome that is closer to the efficient ideal that would result from perfect competition. Nonetheless, anomalous situations aside, those engaged in law and economics often assume that economic systems are smooth, in the mathematical sense that if the change in independent variables is sufficiently small, then the change in the ultimate economic state will not be great. I implicitly use this premise in making the statement that a small deviation from competition is unlikely to drive the outcome far from the efficient ideal.

Suggested Additional Reading

Howard Beales, et al., *The Efficient Regulation of Consumer Information*, 24 J. LAW. & ECON. 491 (1981).

Stephen Breyer, REGULATION AND ITS REFORM (1982).

Harold Demsetz, *Why Regulate Utilities?* 11 J. LAW & ECON. 55 (1968).

Edwin Mansfield, MICROECONOMICS: THEORY AND APPLICATIONS 543-567 (1994).

6
Uncertainty, Risk and Insurance

Thus far we have discussed choices by consumers and producers assuming that they knew with certainty the outcome of their choices. For example, we assumed that if a producer decided to invest in the manufacture of some good, it could calculate the profit it would make by doing so. In reality, the future is highly uncertain. When individuals make investments they do not know for sure what return they will receive. We need to know how consumers act when future payoffs or outcomes are uncertain.

A. Probability Distributions of Outcomes and Risk

Suppose, for example, that when you graduate from law school, you have a choice of jobs. A good friend and classmate has asked you to start your own law firm. That is a risky venture. If it works out, you figure you could make $100,000 a year. But you also figure there is only a 50-50 chance that you will succeed. If you don't succeed, you expect to earn $10,000 a year. Your alternative is to work for a big law firm in town. You know that the firm will pay you $50,000 a year. Which job will you take? Economists cannot predict in the abstract what your answer, or the answer of any individual will be. The answer will depend on your attitude toward risk. But we can learn the tools for analyzing attitudes toward risk, and how individuals might act given a certain attitude.

1. *Probability distributions of outcomes*

We start by characterizing an uncertain future outcome by a distribution of payoffs or values that may occur with a probability associated with each value. That is, an individual facing an uncertain outcome from a decision can describe that outcome as a set of pairs of numbers, the second number being a possible value that might result, and the first number being the probability that that value will occur. Because one of the possible values must occur in the future, these probabilities must add up to 1. Such a set will generally look like:

$$\{(p_1, V_1), (p_2, V_2), \ldots (p_n, V_n)\}$$

where

$$p_1 + p_2 + \ldots + p_n = 1$$

Thus, in our example above, the yearly distribution associated with starting your own practice would be characterized as $\{(½,\$100,000),(½,\$10,000)\}$ and the yearly distribution of working for the firm would be $\{(1,\$50,000)\}$.

2. *Expected value and risk*

There are two attributes of any uncertain outcome that will influence how individuals value the distribution associated with that outcome. The first is the expected value of the distribution. Expected value is the average value of the outcomes that would result if the individual were able

70 MICROECONOMIC PREDICATES TO LAW AND ECONOMICS

to repeat her choice over and over. The expected value is equal to the sum of the probability of each possible value multiplied by its probability. In more precise mathematical terms:

$$E.V. = p_1 \cdot V_1 + p_2 \cdot V_2 + \ldots + p_n \cdot V_n$$

The expected yearly value of starting a practice with your friend would then be ½·$100,000 + ½·$10,000 = $55,000. The expected value of taking the law firm job would be 1·$50,000 = $50,000.[18] The second attribute of any probability distribution is its risk. The risk is related to the spread or dispersion of the probability distribution. The wider the spread of possible values, the greater the risk associated with the future outcome.[19]

It is imperative that you understand that risk is entirely independent of expected value. For example consider two possible investments. The first promises possible returns that may vary from 5% to 15% with an expected return of 10%. The second promises a certain loss of 5%. Although no rational economic actor would invest in the second venture, that venture is less risky than the first because its outcome is certain. The reason that no person would invest in it is because its expected return is negative. The crucial point, however, is that the first distribution, although preferable, is more risky. Frequently, one can tell by simply eye-balling distributions of potential outcomes which involves the greater risk. Graphs of normal distributions with different levels of risk and different expected values are plotted in Figure 38.

If two value distributions exhibit equal risk, consumers will prefer that distribution with the greater expected value. This is a simple corollary of the basic economic assumption that consumers prefer a market-basket with more rather than less of any good. If two value distributions exhibit different levels of risk, however, which one the consumer will prefer will depend on the consumer's individual attitude toward risk (*i.e.* does the consumer dislike risk and, if so, how much?)

B. Expected Utility

We can study how a consumer will treat risk by creating a von Neumann-Morgenstern utility function for the consumer. Such a function assigns a utility value that the consumer places on every level of value or wealth that she can achieve with certainty. We can designate this function as U(V). The function is defined in such a way that for any value distribution, the consumer acts to maximize "expected utility." Expected utility is defined as the expected value of the utilities associated with each value in the distribution. That is:

---

[18] Technically, the set of possible outcomes could include all values between two numbers, say all values between $10,000 and $100,000. The probability associated with each value would then be a "probability density" or weighting such that although the probability of achieving any one value was 0, the "sum" (or more technically integral) of the infinite set of possible values equals 1, and the sum of the probability distribution at a particular value multiplied by that value gives the expected value.

[19] In a course on law and economics, it is not necessary that you know how to calculate the risk of a given outcome distribution precisely. But for those who want to know (perhaps those who will go into corporate finance, for which measures of risk become crucial) the risk is proportional to the variance of the distribution, which is given by:

$$Var = p_1 \cdot (V_1 - E.V.)^2 + \ldots + p_n \cdot (V_n - E.V.)^2$$

Distribution of Potential Values Exhibiting Different Levels of Risk and Different Expected Values

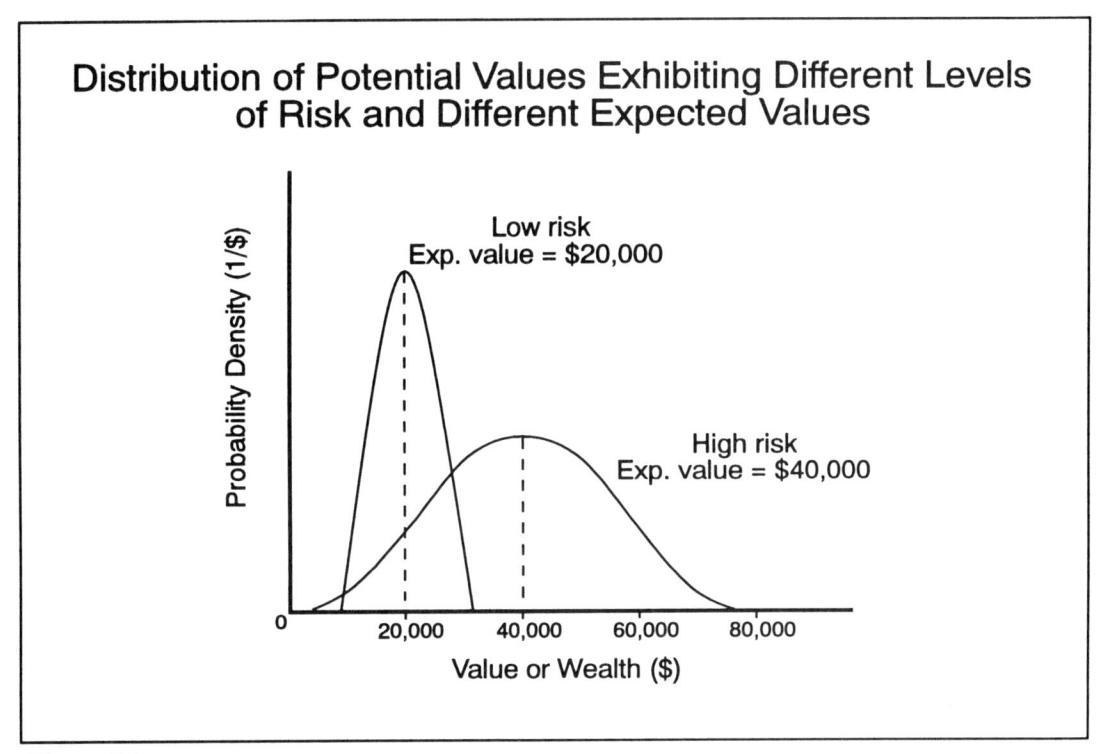

Figure 38

$$\text{Expected Utility (E.U.)} = p_1 \cdot U(V_1) + \ldots + p_n \cdot U(V_n)$$

The nature of the consumers' preferences can be shown by noting that if a distribution consists of two potential outcomes, then the expected utility for the distribution lies along the straight line connecting the points on the von Neumann-Morgenstern utility function for the values of the two outcomes. This demonstrates that a risk-neutral individual—a person who values uncertain outcomes at their expected value regardless of risk— has a straight line for her utility function. It also explains why the utility function for the risk averse individual is concave downward. If a person's utility function is concave downward, then the line connecting any two points on the curve lies below the utility curve. Since points along the line specify the utility of the risky distributions with two possible outcomes, and the curve itself specifies the utility for certain outcomes, this means that, for any expected value of a distribution, the expected utility is lower if the distribution includes multiple possible outcomes (*i.e.*, is risky). By a similar argument, we could show that the utility function for a risk preferrer is concave upward. The von Neumann-Morgenstern utility functions for risk averse and risk preferring consumers are illustrated in Figure 39.

Utility Functions for Risk Averse and Risk Preferring Individuals
Distribution {(1/2,V1),(1/2,V2)}

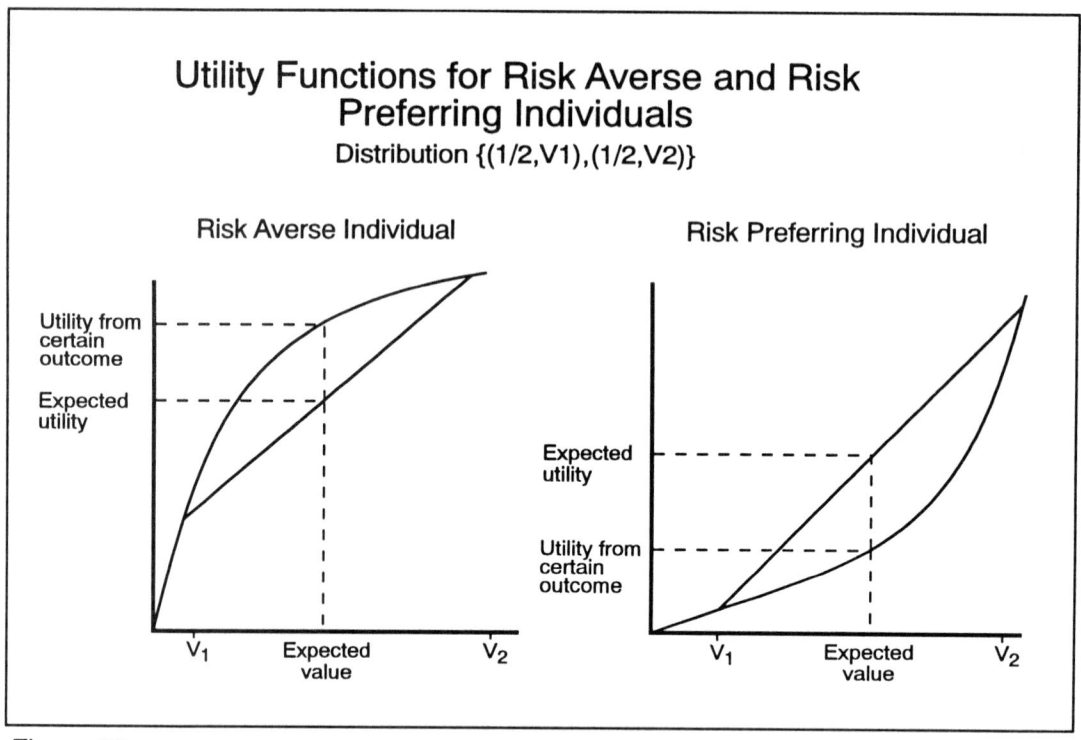

Figure 39

A person's certainty equivalent for a value distribution is the value of the certain outcome from which the individual derives the same utility as she does from the distribution. On our graph of the von Neumann-Morgenstern utility function, the certainty equivalent is found by drawing a horizontal line from the point representing the expected utility of the distribution to the utility function and then drawing a line down to the x-axis. A related concept is the person's "risk premium" associated with a distribution; the risk premium is the difference between the expected value of the distribution and the person's certainty equivalent. The risk premium represents the amount that the individual discounts the value of an uncertain outcome due to risk. The certainty equivalent and risk premium for a risk averse person facing a wealth distribution with two possible outcomes are illustrated in Figure 40.

Most people are risk averse. There are both economic and psychological reasons for this. Economically, we can see from the utility function for the risk averse person that the marginal utility from each additional dollar decreases. This makes intuitive sense: for a poor person another dollar may be the difference between going hungry and eating, while for a wealthy person, another dollar may make little real difference her life. Psychologically, people tend to get used to what they have. They are loathe to give up what they have now with certainty for an unsure future promise. Thus, to the extent that certainty of a future outcome allows a person to budget it and to get used to thinking of the value as already accrued, uncertain outcomes are less desirable.[20]

Certainty Equivalent and Risk Premium

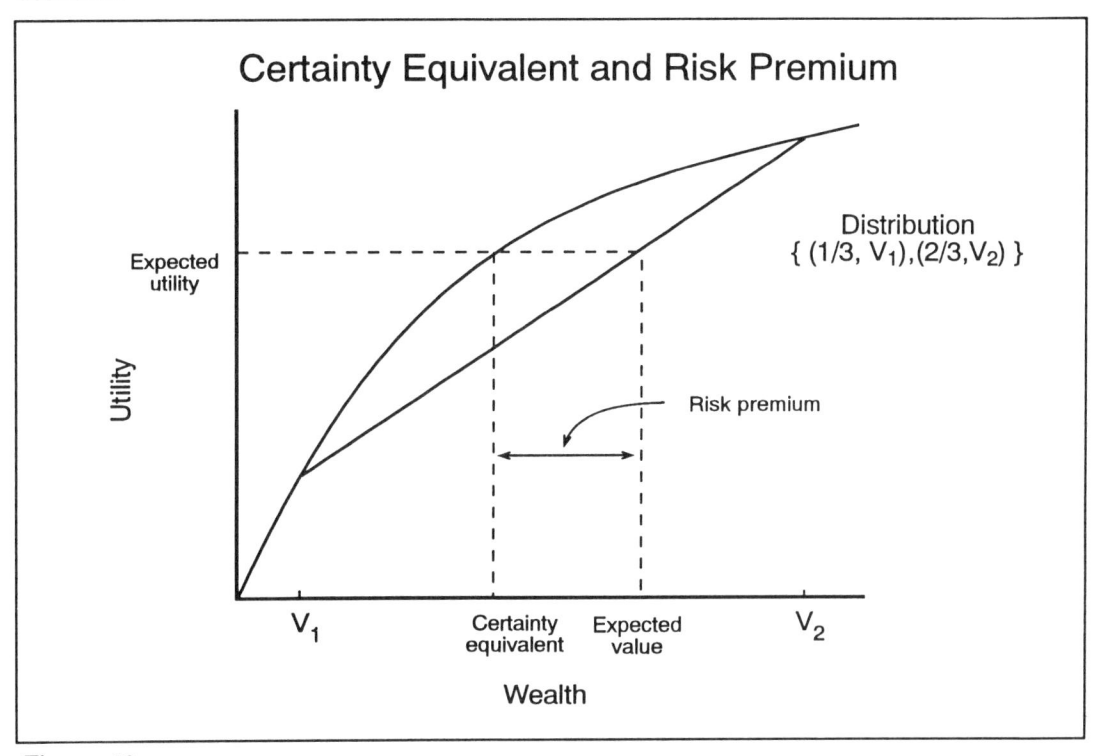

Figure 40

C. Insurance

Risk imposes a real economic opportunity cost on society. Risk averse individuals are less well off when they face risks, and would pay real dollars to avoid having to bear risks. Individuals often can and do avoid some risks by purchasing insurance. To understand how insurance allows individuals to avoid risks consider the following hypothetical. Suppose I value my house at $100,000. If it were to burn down, I would value it at $0. There is some small probability of this occurring, say 0.1%. Then my expected value of owning the house is

---

[20] Economists usually assume that individuals are always risk averse. But the psychology of how people treat various options available to them is complex. Whether a person seeks a risky venture may depend on how the person frames the outcomes. If the person considers a positive albeit uncertain outcome as something which they already have, they may be loathe to give up the opportunity for this outcome. *See* Daniel Kahneman & Amos Tversky, *Prospect Theory: An Analysis of Decision Under Risk*, 47 ECONOMETRICA 263 (1979). Individuals also compartmentalize outcomes into different "mental accounts." Thus a person who won $1000 at black-jack in Las Vegas one day may be willing to risk it at the tables the next day, even though she would never risk that much of "her other money." As the phrase in quotation marks suggests, because the money was won gambling the person considers it available for future gambling. *See* Richard H. Thaler & Eric J. Johnson, *Gambling with the House Money and Trying to Break Even: The Effects of Prior Outcomes on Risky Choice*, 36 MGMT. SCI. 643 (1990).

$99,900. Suppose further that my certainty equivalent for this risky future is $99,000, and that I can fully insure my house against fire for $500. If I were to purchase insurance, and subsequently my house burns down, I would receive a $100,000 insurance payment. Thus, whether or not my house burns down, my value from the house stays at $100,000 and my wealth (which is decreased because of the $500 payment for insurance) stays at $99,500. In other words, with the insurance my future economic outcome becomes a certain (*i.e.* risk free) value of $99,500. In this scenario I will purchase the insurance because a certain value of $99,500 exceeds the $99,000 certainty equivalent of the risky (*i.e.* uninsured) situation.

It is crucial to understand that the reduction of risk by insurance is not a wealth transfer from the insurance company to the policy-holder. Rather it is a reduction in the risk society bears as a whole. The insurance company does not face the risks that the individual did even though the company agreed to make the individual whole. This is because, statistically, if one is exposed repeatedly to similar risks, the relative deviation of the actual value one experiences from the expected value decreases. For instance, in the example above, there is a 0.1% chance that my house will burn down. If it does, this represents a loss of my entire value in the house. Suppose now that the insurance company insures 1,000,000 houses of the same value with the same probability of burning down. The insurance company will expect 1000 houses to burn down. The actual number will vary, but it will not vary by much. Perhaps at best only 950 will burn down, and at worst 1050 will burn down. Thus the insurance company can count on the insurance benefits it pays out to vary between $95,000,000 and $105,000,000, a difference of $10,000,000. This difference, however, represents only 1/10,000 of the total value of houses insured. The insurance company could charge a premium of only $105 and **be certain** that it will cover its obligation to pay for houses that do burn down.

1. *The moral hazard problem*

Although insurance is a good institution for increasing social wealth, it creates some of its own problems. If the insured is really indifferent between the value of the house and the insurance payment if the house burns down, she has no incentive to take due care against it burning down. The insured may decide to leave the fireplace burning while she goes out to dinner, whereas she would never do that if she bore the risk of the house burning down. This in turn may change the probability that the house will burn down. This is known as the "moral hazard" problem. If the insured's behavior can affect the risk of loss, insurance takes away her incentive to take due care. She will then act inefficiently carelessly, unnecessarily decreasing expected social wealth. Insurance companies use deductibles or refuse to insure the full value of some items to give the insured some incentive to continue to take care.

2. *The adverse selection problem*

Another problem with insurance is "adverse selection." The insurance company may be unable to differentiate between high risk and low risk situations. It must price to cover all the risks to which it exposes itself by selling the insurance. But, individuals in low risk situations, who would tend to have a small risk premium, might not find it worth the price to insure against their risks. Only those facing high risks will insure. The risk for those who insure will be greater than for the population as a whole, driving the cost of insurance up further. This scenario will repeat itself until insurance gets too costly for anyone, or the only individuals buying it are those facing very high risks. In our house example, suppose 2% of the population of homeowners are pyromaniacs. The probability that a pyromaniac's house will burn down is close to 100%. The expected loss per house will then rise to about 2.1% or $2,100. To cover this, the insurance company will have to charge at least this amount for premiums. But, according to our assumption that the non-pyromaniac homeowner puts a $99,000 certainty equivalent on the uninsured house, such a homeowner will not pay more than $1,000 for insurance. Thus, only the pyromaniacs, whose risky behavior makes selling them insurance adverse to the company, will actually purchase insurance at $2,100. If only pyromaniacs buy insurance, however, the insurance company would soon learn from its actuarial experience that the percentage of insured homes that burn down is close to 100%. To cover its payments it will have to raise its premiums to the value of each house. At this price even the pyromaniacs will stop purchasing insurance. Thus, adverse selection, if sufficiently extreme, can completely destroy the market for insurance. Insurance companies combat adverse selection by trying to ascertain as precisely as possible the risks each insured poses and to price insurance in accordance with such risks.

3. *Example: Joe's drinking problem, the benefits of insurance, and the need for "deductibles"*

The benefits of insurance, the concept of moral hazard and the effect of deductibles is illustrated by the following hypothetical example. Suppose the probability of an individual's health problems is a function of how much he drinks. In particular, assume that the cost of any hospital stay is $10,000, but the probability of being hospitalized varies with the amount of drinking. In addition assume that all individuals are risk averse and put a risk premium on the uncertain prospect of having to pay for a hospital stay equal to the expected cost of such a stay (*i.e.* if the expected cost of a stay is $600, an individual would pay up to $1200 for insurance to cover hospital costs). The following table summarizes the expected costs of a hospital stay as a function of drinking, and the value of the drinks to the individual (net of the direct cost of the drinks).

Drinks per Day	Expected Cost of Hospital Visit	Certainty Equiv. of Expected Hospital Cost	Value of Drinks to the Insured
0	$ 600	$ 1200	$ 0
1	650	1300	130
2	750	1500	240
3	900	1800	290
4	1100	2200	320

Now we can consider how many drinks our average consumer, Joe, will drink and how net social wealth varies under different insurance scenarios. If insurance for health care were not available, and assuming Joe acts as an economically rational individual, he will imbibe one drink per day. Under this scenario, Joe bears all the cost of drinking. Hence he will see a net cost of $1170 if he imbibes once a day ($1300 due to expected hospital cost plus his risk premium minus the $130 value of drinking). Drinking any more or less will decrease Joe's net benefit. In addition, overall social wealth is -$1170. Note that because Joe bears all costs and derives all benefits from drinking, social wealth is just the negative of Joe's net costs.

Suppose now that Joe can purchase "perfect insurance." Such insurance pays for all of Joe's hospital costs, and its price is equal to the administrative costs of providing such insurance plus the expected costs of claims that insurance company will see because it insures Joe. Because the insurance is perfect, we assume that the insurance company can costlessly determine how much Joe drinks and write a contract that reflects this level of drinking. Assume for the sake of concreteness that administrative costs are $100. Then the price of insurance to Joe would be $700 if he does not drink, $750 if he has one drink per day, $850 if he has two drinks daily, $1000 if he has three drinks, and $1200 if he has four drinks. In this case Joe will be indifferent between going to the hospital and remaining healthy since the insurance company compensates him perfectly for a hospital stay. Joe will now imbibe two drinks per day, as that minimizes his net cost at $610 (the cost of insurance minus his benefit from drinking). Because perfect insurance internalizes all the cost of drinking to Joe, again the overall social wealth is the negative of Joe's cost, -$610. A crucial point of this scenario is that society is better off because the availability of insurance has eliminated the social cost of risk.

Consider next an imperfect insurance scenario. The administrative costs of insurance increase, but the insurance company cannot determine Joe's level of drinking at all. Hence it will have to price insurance the same for all people regardless of their level of drinking. In order to cover its costs, assume the insurance company prices insurance at $1200 (which covers their costs even for individuals who drink four drinks a day). Joe will purchase the insurance because its cost is equal to the effective cost he sees for hospital stays if uninsured. With insurance, however, Joe bears none of the cost of drinking. Hence he will drink four drinks daily. Overall social wealth under this scenario will be -$880 ($1100 in expected hospital costs plus $100 in insurance administrative costs minus the $320 benefit from drinking). Although the social costs under this scenario are less than without insurance, the imperfection in pricing insurance results in inefficient behavior by Joe and a loss of $370 in social wealth from the perfect insurance scenario. This loss results because Joe's lack of concern about the costs of his drinking creates a moral hazard for the insurance company.

Finally, suppose that the insurance company, concerned about the moral hazard problem, agrees to pay 80% of the costs of any hospital stay. It prices this imperfect insurance at $880 (again, enough for the company to cover its costs even if Joe has four drinks a day). Joe will buy the insurance and then see a risk premium for the 20% of the costs that he will have to pay if he goes to the hospital. A little arithmetic leads to the conclusion that Joe will drink two drinks a day, and see a net cost of $940 (a $150 direct cost of the hospital stay, plus a $150 risk premium plus $880 for insurance minus a $240 benefit of drinking). At this level of drinking, overall social wealth will be -$760. This is worse than the outcome under perfect insurance: the inability of the insurance company to determine Joe's level of drinking has prompted the company to offer incomplete insurance which leaves some risk on Joe. Given the inability of the company to price its insurance perfectly, however, the use of the 20% co-payment increases social wealth over the level obtained with complete but imperfect insurance. The co-payment does so because it forces Joe to retain an incentive to curb his drinking. (Note—Joe drinks only two drinks, the optimal level even with perfect insurance). In other words, the co-payment increases social wealth by reducing the moral hazard problem.

Suggested Additional Reading

Edwin Mansfield, MICROECONOMICS: THEORY AND APPLICATIONS 141-170 (1994).

Mark V. Pauly, *The Economics of Moral Hazard: Comment*, 58 AM. ECON. REV. 531 (1968).

Amos Tversky & Daniel Kahneman, *Rational Choice and the Framing of Decisions*, 59 J. BUS. S251 (1986); *reprinted in* THE LIMITS OF RATIONALITY 60 (Karen S. Cook & Margaret Levi, eds., 1990).

7
Choices Over Time—Decisions About Lending And Investing

In our discussion of risk, we considered uncertain future payouts, and we examined how uncertainty affected the value of a future payout. We did not, however, consider how time itself might affect the value of that payout or, in other words, how we should compare the value of a payout today with the same payout several years hence. Yet, most people are aware, at least indirectly, that "time is money." The need to compute the present value of a future payout arises in almost every aspect of law and economics. It arises directly, for example, when a judge has to award a present sum that compensates a tort victim for future lost wages. But it also arises in evaluation of the efficiency of many legal doctrines. For instance, the wisdom of the doctrine of "coming to the nuisance" might well depend on the value of the present day use of property relative to the value of future uses with which the present day use might interfere. To consider the present value of a future payout, we must introduce the notion of the time value of money.

A. The Time Value of Money

The time value of money arises because most individuals will not forego present use of their wealth in return for a future payout that will merely provide the same level of goods and services that the individuals could purchase at the present time. Although economists do not address why individuals value present use more than future use, for risk averse individuals this preference for present consumption is consistent with the uncertainty that necessarily surrounds future consumption. An individual who defers present consumption for the promise of a future payout may not be alive when the payout comes due. Even if she is alive, the individual's personal circumstances might have changed in ways that alter the value of the payout to her; in the extreme she may have decided to avoid the commercialism of the modern world and become a hermit for whom the ability to purchase material goods is not important. Additionally, the state of the economy might alter the value of the future payout: if inflation runs rampant, the individual may be able to purchase fewer goods than she initially anticipated, while if inflation is low, she might be able to purchase more than she anticipated. The key point is that the value to an individual of the future payout of even an assured sum of money is more uncertain than the value of that sum of money today. All else being equal, the risk averse individual will thus attach a lower value to the future payout than to a present payout.

1. *The interest rate for borrowing and lending*

The relationship of value of a present payout to a future payout will vary from individual to individual. Yet, the economics of the time value of money allows the assignment of a universal interest rate by which future payouts must be discounted. To understand how we can assign such a universal rate, we need to analogize the choice between consumption of wealth

80 MICROECONOMIC PREDICATES TO LAW AND ECONOMICS

today versus consumption in the future to an individual's choice between the consumption of two goods.

Just as an individual's relative preference for a good like food decreases as the individual gets more and more of the good, the same is true of present consumption. An individual whose present desires are fairly well sated, but who is unsure of how she will fare in the future, is likely to choose to set aside some of her present wealth for future consumption. She can do so by lending money in return for a promise of future repayment of the money with interest. The more she sets aside, the less money she has to meet her present needs, and the greater the interest she will demand for setting aside still more of her wealth. By the same argument, a consumer who has little money at present, but expects to have more than enough in the future will pay a fairly high price to borrow to allow her to purchase goods and services today. As she borrows more and more, her need for present consumption decreases, and she will be willing to pay less and less interest for the privilege of using money today that she will repay tomorrow.

Thus, we can represent a consumers's choice of whether to borrow or lend money by using her indifference curves for present and future consumption. The budget line then reflects the going "price" of money—that is, the interest rate that individuals will demand in order to forego present consumption for future consumption. The consumer can borrow or lend to reach any point along this line, and thereby adjust present consumption versus future consumption to maximize her level of satisfaction. Just as the market, through supply and demand, sets the relative price of goods, it can also set an equilibrium interest rate for borrowing and lending money.

Figure 41 illustrates this for a consumer, Barb. If Barb neither lends nor borrows money, she will be at point A; she will earn and consume $60,000 this year and $44,000 next year. The budget line has a slope of -1.1, which means that the market has established the annual interest rate at 10%. According to the indifference curves shown, Barb maximizes her utility by lending $10,000 this year and receiving back $11,000 next year ($10,000 x 1.1). By doing so, she reaches point B; she consumes $50,000 of her wealth this year and $55,000 next year.

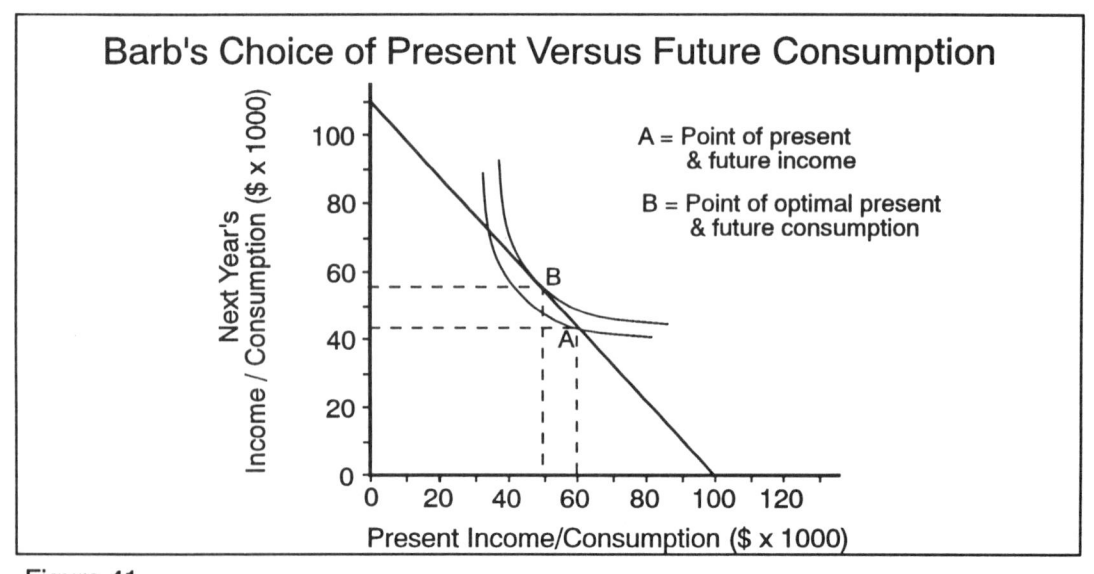

Figure 41

2. *The present value of future payouts*

We can use this interest rate to compare the value of a future payout of money to the value of the money today. Such a comparison is usually done by computing the present value of the future payout—the amount of money today that would be equivalent in value to the future payout. If the going annual interest rate for a risk free loan is **r**,[21] then the minimum payout that a lender will demand in a year in return for lending a principal **PV** will be (1+r)**PV**. This is the payout that makes the lender indifferent between lending and not lending. If we denote this payout as **D**, then we can express **PV** in terms of **D** as **PV** = **D** ÷ (1+r). The fact, however, that the lender is indifferent between making the loan and keeping the principal, means that the principal **PV** is precisely the present value of a payout **D** distributed one year hence. In other words,

$$\mathbf{PV} = \mathbf{D} \div (1+\mathbf{r})$$

represents the equation for the present value of a payment of **D** one year from the present, if the market interest rate per year is **r**.

The expression for the present value of a payout several years hence can be derived by repeating the steps used to obtain the formula for a payout one year from the present. If the payout, **D**, occurs two years hence, then its value one year hence is **D** ÷ (1+r). A payout with this value one year hence will have a present value equal to 1/(1+r) times this, or **D** ÷ (1+r)². More generally, the present value of a payout of **D** n-years hence is **D** ÷ (1+r)ⁿ. Finally, we can generalize the expression for present value to cover an annuity for n-years—that is, a payout of **D** every year for the next n years. The present value is merely the sum of the present value of each yearly payout, or

$$\mathbf{PV} = \mathbf{D}/(1+\mathbf{r}) + \mathbf{D}/(1+\mathbf{r})^2 + \ldots + \mathbf{D}/(1+\mathbf{r})^n \text{ [22]}$$

The easiest way to understand how to calculate present value is to consider an example. Suppose the going interest rate for a risk free loan is 10% per year. Suppose further that the lender expects to be paid back $10,000 precisely one year hence. Then the present value of the payout is simply $10,000 ÷ 1.1 = $9,090.91. That means that a lender would not lend more than $9,090.91 in return for a guaranty of a $10,000 repayment a year after the loan, and a borrower would not repay more than $10,000 a year after a loan of $9,090.91.

3. *Investment to produce goods in the future*

In discussing the market for intertemporal transfers of money, we considered only the

---

[21] Thus far, we have only considered future payouts that are certain to occur and of a certain value. We will consider the effect of the riskiness of a future payout on its present value later in this chapter.

[22] There is a special case of this equation of particular significance for those studying corporate finance. A corporation is often thought of as having an infinite life. Its value should equal the value of its dividend stream over its life. If the dividend is expected to remain constant at **D**, then the value of the corporation should be given by the formula for the present value of an infinite annuity. The equation contains an infinite number of summands, but sums to the nice finite expression, **PV** = **D** ÷ r.

consumer side. There is also a producer side to this market. The producer side is represented by investors who do not merely trade present for future income, but rather use present wealth (capital and labor) to produce goods in the future.

We can define an investment possibility curve analogous to the production possibility curve that we used to discuss the mix of goods that the market will produce. An investment possibility curve will indicate how much future wealth investors can create by foregoing the use of resources that can produce present wealth. Recall that, absent market imperfections, we posited that the production possibility curve would be concave to the origin. This reflected the assumption that as more and more resources are devoted to producing a certain good, the amount of additional resources needed to produce the next unit of the good increases. The same assumption makes sense for investment in production of future goods.

In an economy dedicated to the production of present goods, the devotion of a small quantity of resources to producing goods in the future is likely to result in a significant increase in future wealth. At some point, as more and more resources are taken from present production and devoted to future production, the marginal rate at which such resources can produce future wealth will fall. First, if there is a flood of production of future goods, the value of such goods relative to the value of present goods will fall. Moreover, at some point without production of present goods (including food and leisure) those who labor to produce future goods will starve or become exhausted. Thus, there is good reason to presume that, in a well operating economy, the curve depicting the trade-off between producing present goods and future goods will look like an ordinary production possibility curve.

Having posited a concave investment possibility curve, we can borrow from our analysis of the relation between consumption and production of ordinary goods to discuss what the equilibrium will look like in a competitive market trading present wealth for future wealth. Because a competitive market is allocatively efficient, investors will continue to increase future production until the marginal rate of product transformation between present and future wealth equals the consumers' marginal rate of substitution of present for future income. The marginal rate of product transformation for investors, however, is merely one plus the marginal rate of return investors achieve on their investments, and the marginal rate of substitution for consumers is merely one plus the interest rate they demand for lending money. Hence, if the market for investment and lending is competitive, then investors will continue to invest in future production until their marginal rate of return on their investment equals the interest rate that those who provide capital demand for the use of their money.

This seemingly uncontroversial conclusion nonetheless is helpful in clarifying why one discounts future costs and benefits to present value before assessing whether an action with such costs and benefits is wealth enhancing. For example, some environmentalists have asserted that in determining whether a project is cost-beneficial (*i.e.* wealth maximizing) it is not correct to discount the cost of future health or environmental harm to present value. They argue, for instance, that the value of human life to a future generation must be the same as the value of a life today. There is no reason to believe that individuals in the future will derive any less satisfaction from living than do people today. Despite the appeal of this argument, as a matter of economics, it is wrong. The reason that a life today is worth more than one in fifty years is not because individuals today will derive any more satisfaction from life than will people in the future, but rather because the resources needed to save a life could be invested in production of future wealth (perhaps saving more than one life in the future). The fact that the market demands interest for consumers to delay their present consumption means that investors will not invest in a project unless it is expected to increase the totality of goods and services available in the future. Thus, the relationship between the interest demanded by those who provide capital for investment and the return on investment in future wealth clarifies that, in fact, future health and environmental harms, like any cost, should be discounted to present value.[23]

B. Risk and Return

Thus far, we have discussed the time value of money, and the discount rate used for calculation of future payout, only for payouts that are certain to occur at a specified time and at a specified amount. In fact, because of the uncertainty of future events, future payouts are frequently uncertain. When an individual purchases stock, he might expect a certain yearly dividend based on the company's historic performance and its present economic circumstances. But over time, those circumstances can change, and the expected payout may be more or less than expected. In other words, we need to incorporate the risk associated with the uncertainty about the amount of future payouts into our calculation of the present value of an investment.

Most individuals, in their roles as investors, seem to be risk averse. We already know that a risk averse individual will place a certainty equivalent on an uncertain outcome that is less than the expected value of that outcome. Thus, the present value of an uncertain annuity or "income stream" must be discounted to reflect its risky character. We could try to substitute certainty equivalents for the actual expected values of uncertain future payouts. Then each subsequent year's payout will have a value less than that of the previous year to reflect that as the time until the payout increases the uncertainty of the payout also increases. Simply put, because the risk derives from the uncertainty of future events, risk will rise in proportion to the time until the payout. Instead of attaching certainty equivalents to each payout, however, we could simply increase the interest rate that we use to discount the future payout. Doing so will automatically decrease the expected value of payouts far in the future more than those close at hand.

Just as the market for investment sets an equilibrium price (*i.e.* an interest rate) for risk free investments, it can set a unique interest rate for all investments with equal levels of risk. The greater the risk of the investment, the greater the interest rate that the market will demand. The risk an investor sees from a particular venture, however, may not be the risk of that venture considered in isolation. If an individual can invest in two different ventures whose payouts will

---

[23] I do not mean to belittle other economic arguments that caution against destruction of future natural resources. For example, there may be inherent problems with putting a value on human life or natural resources that lead to the assignment of monetary values that are too low. In addition, markets for health and resources are often far from perfectly competitive; if investors do not bear the full cost of their projects (*i.e.* if they impose an external cost) that will certainly skew their calculation of costs and benefits in a way that will lead them to engage in projects that might decrease overall future wealth. Nor do I mean to cast aspersions on non-economic arguments against the destruction of future natural resources. For example, I do not condemn the philosophical contention that today's generation has a moral obligation to preserve a healthful environment and natural resources to allow future generations the same level of autonomy over the kind of world in which they want to live as we presently enjoy. But, although I find this argument interesting, I do not believe it can be asserted as a matter of economic efficiency.

change in different ways in response to external conditions, the risk of the "portfolio" of the two investments will be less than the risk from either investment separately. For example, if one invests in a corn farm in the Midwest of the United States, there is a risk that the weather in the area will be bad, and the yield from the farm will be low. The investor can avoid some of this risk by investing in corn farms all over the world. If the weather in the Midwest is bad, the low yield from crops in that region will drive the price of corn up. Thus, the same external factor that drives the value of the Midwest farm down, will drive the value of the other farms up. Hence, by diversifying his corn portfolio, the investor can avoid some weather related risks.

Unfortunately for the investor (and society), one cannot diversify the portfolio to avoid all weather related risks. The investor must still worry that the weather in every corn producing region is bad, harming yields of corn internationally. The investor may also have to worry that the weather in corn producing regions globally is so good, that the price of corn plummets below that necessary to cover the costs of farming it. The crucial point is that by diversifying one's portfolio of investments, one can decrease risk below the level of the risk of each individual investment, but cannot eliminate risks entirely.

If the market were to reward risks of venture that investors could avoid by diversification, some investors would avoid the risk and offer capital for the venture at a lower rate of return. This would drive the required rate of return on the investment down until the rate reflected that for risk that could not be avoided. Hence, the interest rates for risky ventures reflects only that risk that cannot be avoided by diversification—, so called "systematic" risk. A measure of the systematic risk of an investment is called the β of the investment, and it is only this risk that the market rate of return on the investment reflects.

Suggested Additional Reading

Richard Brealey & Stewart Myers, PRINCIPLES OF CORPORATE FINANCE 10-154 (1981).

Edwin Mansfield, MICROECONOMICS: THEORY AND APPLICATIONS 141-168 (8th ed. 1994).

Burton G. Malkiel, A RANDOM WALK DOWN WALL STREET 215-37 (1990).

8
Strategic Behavior And Game Theory

Traditionally, price theory posits rational economic actors who pursue the maximization of wealth straightforwardly in situations for which the opportunities available to one individual are considered independent of the choices of other individuals. In reality, however, the economic opportunities available to one actor may depend directly on the choices made by another. For example, a person may face the decision whether to enter into a contract that if performed makes her better off. But, the increase in the person's welfare is dependent on the other party not breaching the contract. If the person believes that the other party will breach then she will not enter into the contract, if she believes the other party will perform, then she will. Of course the other party's opportunities to maximize his utility will depend on the willingness of the first party to enter into the contract. Thus, the parties will act strategically. They will act to maximize their wealth given what they expect the other party to do.

Another example for which strategic behavior is important involves the choices of producers in a type of market called an oligopoly. An oligopoly is characterized by a small number of producers who can influence price by their decisions regarding how much to produce, but who cannot unilaterally dictate price. If one producer decides to increase price, the others may decide to follow or not. If all follow, all stand to gain some profits. An individual producer may be able to do even better, however, if it can sell the goods at a lower price without causing a price war.

A. Normal Form Games

To analyze situations involving strategic behavior we need to study a branch of microeconomics called "game theory." A game involves a set of players, each of which is presented with potential choices, and a "payoff" that corresponds to each set of choices by the players. A player's strategy is a specification of the choices the player would make for every possible set of choices by the other players. Thus, a strategy for an oligopolist may be to maintain existing prices if other producers in the market do not change their prices, but to match any price changes of other producers. By assuming that players are wealth maximizers, a player would analyze the payoffs of all her potential strategies with the hope of predicting which payoff will actually occur (or at least limiting the actual payoffs to a small subset of all possible outcomes).

The simplest games involve two players and a small number of choices. Often these games can be modeled by creating a table of the potential payoffs from all possible strategies. When the game is specified in this manner, it is called a "normal form game." The entries in the table are two numbers, the payoff to player one followed by the payoff to player two. The well known game of the prisoner's dilemma is a good example. There are two players in this game. Each player is charged with the commission of a crime that the prosecutor believes both perpetrated together. The prosecutor takes each suspect into a separate room and offers each a reduced sentence if he will turn state's evidence against the other. If the suspect turns state's evidence and his compatriot does not, the "snitch" gets to go free and the compatriot gets 10 years. If both turn state's evidence against each other, however, the prosecutor will recommend 7 years for each. Finally, if neither snitches, then the prosecutor only has a 10% chance of convicting either suspect, so both get an expected sentence of 1 year. The game can be represented by the following table of payoffs (since payoffs are measured by expected years in prison, the higher the number the worse the outcome, so the payoffs are indicated by negative numbers):

PAYOFFS FOR THE PRISONER'S DILEMMA
(expected years in prison x -1)

	Suspect 2 remains silent	Suspect 2 snitches
Suspect 1 remains silent	-1, -1	-10, 0
Suspect 1 snitches	0, -10	-7, -7

We can determine the outcome of this game by looking at the choices facing player 1. Regardless of whether player 2 remains silent or snitches, player 1 is better off if he snitches. A strategy like this—which makes the player better off regardless of what the other players do—is called a dominant strategy. A player that seeks to maximize wealth will always play a dominant strategy. By the same argument, snitching is a dominant strategy for player 2 as well. Thus, the outcome to this game is that each suspect will snitch and the prosecutor will be able to get 7 years for both of them.

B. Nash Equilibrium

Not all games will contain dominant strategies. To solve games without such strategies, we need to introduce the concept of Nash Equilibrium. Nash Equilibrium is a generalization of the notion of market equilibrium that we introduced when discussing competitive markets. An outcome to a game is a Nash Equilibrium if no player can improve their payoff given the choices of the other players that lead to the outcome. Essentially, the idea behind Nash Equilibrium is that once the players play strategies that lead to the equilibrium, no player will decide to change his strategy. Thus, once the equilibrium is reached, the system or game will remain at the equilibrium. Games may have one Nash equilibrium, several Nash equilibria, or even no Nash equilibrium.[24]

The significance of Nash Equilibrium is that the outcome of any game, to the extent there is a determinate outcome, must be a Nash equilibrium. If it were not then some player could

---

[24] It can be shown that the simple two person games that we consider in this section have at least one Nash equilibrium.

improve his payoff by changing his strategy, given the strategies that the other players have chosen. Being a wealth maximizer (*i.e.* rational economic actor), that player will change his strategy. But that will move the outcome away from the posited outcome. The converse, however, is not true. Not every Nash equilibrium will be the outcome to the game. For games with multiple equilibria, we would have to decide if the parties are more likely to reach one of the equilibria than the others.

The following game involving reliance and breach of contract illustrates how the concept of Nash equilibrium can help us to predict the outcome of the game. Players 1 and 2 have already entered the contract. Player 1, the promisee, first must decide the extent to which she will rely on the contract. If Player 2 performs the contract, then greater reliance results in a greater payoff for Player 1. But, if Player 2 breaches, then greater reliance results in a greater loss. Knowing what Player 1 has decided, Player 2 must decide whether to perform or breach the contract. If he performs, he gets the same payoff regardless of the level of Player 1's reliance. But if he breaches, Player 1 will find it beneficial to sue only if she relied greatly on performance. Thus, Player 2 is best off if he breaches and Player 1 relied slightly, but is worst off if he breaches and Player 1 relied greatly. The following table is the normal form for the game:

NORMAL FORM OF THE RELIANCE-BREACH GAME

	Player 1 relies slightly	Player 1 relies greatly
Player 2 performs	2, 5	8, 5
Player 2 breaches	-2, 6	-5, -5

There are two pure strategy Nash equilibria to this game. One would have Player 1 rely greatly and Player 2 perform. The other would have Player 1 rely slightly and Player 2 breach. Given the normal form of the game, it is impossible to figure with certainty which of the equilibria will occur. But, the numbers would suggest that the equilibrium in which Player 1 relies greatly and Player 2 performs is more likely to occur. Player 1 gains only a $3 advantage by relying slightly even if Player 2 were to breach, but gains a $6 advantage from relying greatly if Player 2 performs. It would seem unlikely that Player 1 would ever rely slightly. In other words, it is unlikely that the players would ever reach the equilibrium of relying slightly and breaching. We will see that there is another way to specify this game, and another approach to solving it that shows that the rely slightly—breach equilibrium will not occur.

C. Extensive Form Games

The other way of specifying games is to specify the players in the game, when each player can act and the choices available to the player when she can act, what the player knows about the actions of the other players at every decision, and the payoffs to each player from each possible combination of actions. A game specified in this manner is called an "extensive form game." Usually the decision points are designated by nodes, with lines leading to the next step in the game. Thus a line from a node can either lead to a payoff or a decision node for another player. When a player is not aware of a previous decision made by other players, the decision nodes representing the possible actions available to the player are connected by a dashed line. The extensive form of the prisoners dilemma game is illustrated below.

EXTENSIVE FORM OF THE PRISONERS DILEMMA
(Payoffs in Expected Years in Prison x -1)

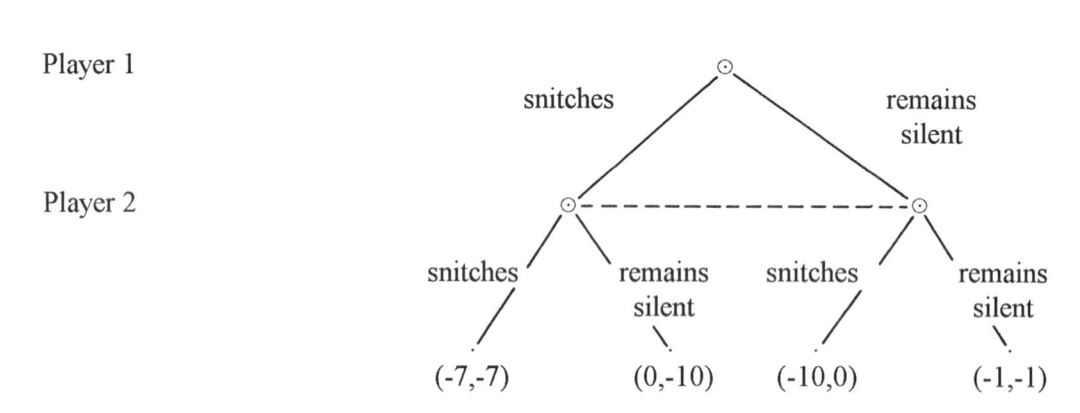

Player 1

    snitches   remains silent

Player 2

snitches   remains silent   snitches   remains silent

(-7,-7)   (0,-10)   (-10,0)   (-1,-1)

One way to solve extensive form games is to work backwards. Thus, we begin by analyzing the choices of Player 2. Although Player 2 does not know Player 1's decision (as indicated by the dashed line connecting Player 2's decision nodes) regardless of Player 1's decision, Player 2 is better off by snitching. Player 1, figuring this out, can then convert the game into one which attaches payoffs directly to his decision. The simplified game facing Player 1 would look like:

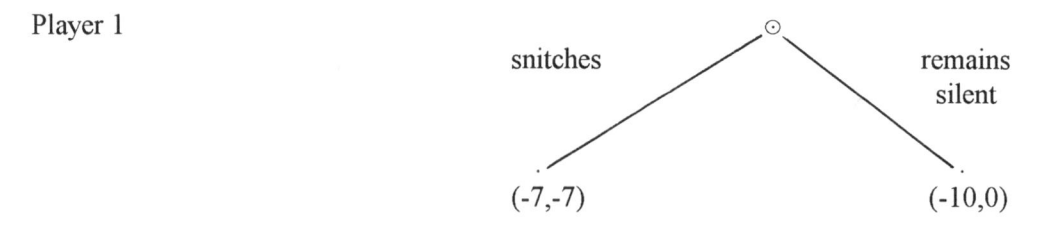

Player 1

snitches   remains silent

(-7,-7)   (-10,0)

Faced with this simple game, Player 1 maximizes his payoff by snitching. Thus both Player 2 and Player 1 will snitch.

Working backwards merely gave us the same solution that we had already reached in the prisoner's dilemma. Applying it to the reliance-breach game we looked at earlier, however, shows that it is a more powerful tool for solving games than is the tool of merely finding Nash equilibria. The extensive form of the reliance-breach game looks as follows:

EXTENSIVE FORM OF THE RELIANCE-BREACH GAME

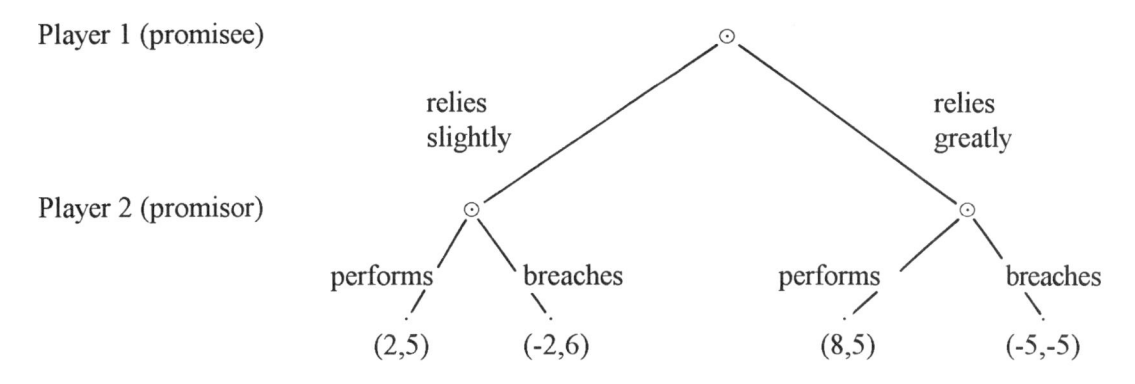

Player 1 (promisee)

                                     relies   relies
                                     slightly   greatly

Player 2 (promisor)

                     performs   breaches   performs   breaches

                      (2,5)   (-2,6)   (8,5)   (-5,-5)

We again begin by analyzing the decision of Player 2, who knows how Player 1 has acted. If Player 1 has relied slightly, then Player 2 will maximize his payoff at $6 by breaching. If Player 1 has relied greatly, Player 2 will maximize his payoff at $5 by performing. Because Player 1 can figure this out, the simplified game she now faces is as follows:

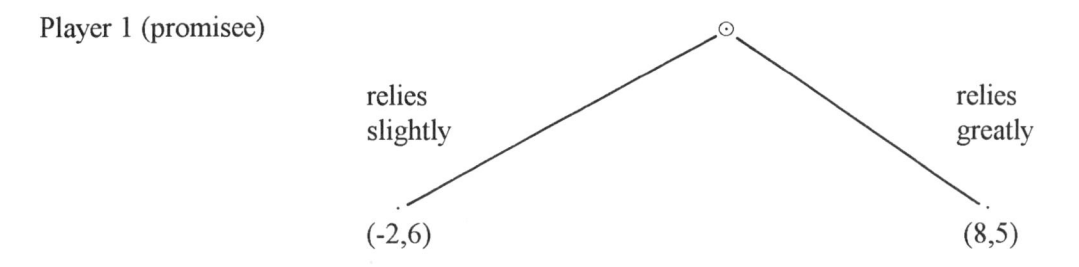

Player 1 (promisee)

                     relies   relies
                     slightly   greatly

                     (-2,6)   (8,5)

Faced with this game, Player 1 will maximize her payoff at $8 by relying greatly. Because she relies greatly, we know from the previous step in the analysis that Player 2 chooses to perform. Hence the outcome to this game is determinate: Player 1 relies greatly and Player 2 performs the contract.

We have merely touched on the rudiments of game theory. Game theory has developed into a very powerful tool for analyzing situations involving strategic behavior. We may run into more complicated games as we discuss various topics in law and economics. But it is probably best to develop any other game theoretic ideas as we need them. In that way they will be more relevant and hence will make more sense to you. For now it suffices that you have the fundamental concepts of the theory, which will allow you to see when it might apply, and to use it to analyze some situations involving strategic behavior.

Suggested Additional Reading

Ian Ayres, *Playing Games with the Law*, 42 STAN. L. REV. 1291 (1990).

Douglas G. Baird, et al., GAME THEORY AND THE LAW (1994).

Avinash K. Dixit & Barry J. Nalebuff, THINKING STRATEGICALLY: THE COMPETITIVE EDGE IN BUSINESS, POLITICS AND EVERYDAY LIFE (1991).

Eric Rasmusen, GAMES AND INFORMATION: AN INTRODUCTION TO GAME THEORY (1989).

9
Coase's Theorem—Efficient Allocation of Legal Entitlements

Thus far we have studied economic theory that, although applicable to legal issues, is also applicable to many other issues that economists address. Coase's Theorem, however, is explicitly law related. It concerns itself with the allocation of legal entitlements and the effect of that allocation on efficient outcomes. This is precisely the thrust of the whole subject of law and economics. As such, technically Coase's Theorem is not "economic background," but rather part and parcel of the subject of law and economics.[25] Nonetheless, the lessons of Coase's Theorem apply to every possible legal rule which we might economically evaluate. Because its applicability is universal, no text on economic predicates to law and economics would be complete without presenting and discussing Coase's Theorem.

Coase's Theorem states that **if transaction costs are zero, then rational economic entities will bargain to an efficient outcome regardless of how legal entitlements are allocated.** Thus, if transactions costs were zero, it would not matter from an efficiency perspective what the law was. As long as the parties were allowed to bargain around the law, they would bargain to reach an economically efficient solution.

Rather than deriving Coase's Theorem in general, it is more instructive to illustrate it with a modification of an example Coase used in his original article presenting the theorem.[26] Consider a train that runs along cropland. When the train runs it emits sparks that occasionally ignite the crops on adjoining land. The following table sums up the costs and benefits of running trains (assuming farmers maintain the same level of crop production).

Number of Trains Daily	Railroad Revenue From Running Trains	Railroad Cost of Running Trains	Cost of Fires Caused by Trains
0	$ 0	$ 0	$ 0
1	200	50	60
2	350	100	120
3	450	150	180
4	490	200	240

---

[25] Coase's Theorem, although law and economics, is sufficiently important to economists to have earned Ronald Coase the Nobel Prize in Economics.

[26] See R. H. Coase, *The Problem of Social Cost*, 3 J. LAW & ECON. 1 (1960).

Assume for the sake of simplicity that the railroad captures the full social wealth of running trains as part of its profits. The social wealth that results from running trains is the railroad's revenue minus the direct cost of running the trains minus the loss due to fires set by the trains. We can then determine that it is socially optimal for the railroad to run 2 trains, as that maximizes social wealth at $130.

To begin, assume that the railroad and the farmers cannot negotiate any enforceable legal agreement. We want to see whether the law should make the railroad pay the cost of fires it causes. If the railroad has the legal entitlement to set fires—that is, is not liable for harm caused by the fires its trains set—then it will ignore the cost of fires and maximize its profits at $300 by running 3 trains. If the railroad is liable for the harm caused by the fires, it will internalize the cost of fires and run 2 trains—the optimal number. Its profits will then be $130. This is just an example of the railroad imposing an external cost; the railroad will produce greater than the socially optimal amount unless the law forces the railroad to internalize the cost of fires.

Coase's insight was to realize that the notion of one user imposing cost on another—here a railroad imposing cost on farmers—was reciprocal. If the railroad has to pay for the harm from fires, one can think of the farmers imposing cost on the railroad by planting crops near the tracks. It follows from this way of conceptualizing the problem that forcing the railroad to internalize the cost of fires means that farmers will impose an external cost on railroads. To illustrate this, in our example suppose further that farmers have a choice of whether to plant additional crops closer to the railroad tracks. Planting such crops will allow the farmers to receive $50 more in profits for their crops, but will double the harm caused by crops burning in fires started by trains.

If the farmers are totally compensated for fires caused by trains, they will not bear any of the extra cost of fires that results from planting extra crops. They will plant the crops and receive the extra $50 in profits. If they plant the extra crops, the railroad will maximize its profits at $30 by running 1 train. Social wealth will be $80 ($30 in railroad profits and $50 in farmer profits). This is $50 less than the level of social wealth that society would achieve if the farmers did not plant the extra crops. Hence, planting extra crops is not socially optimal. As Coase made clear, the farmers will ignore the cost of fires, and like any producer that has externalized costs, will overproduce crops. Hence, the first lesson of Coase's Theorem is that when one speaks of internalizing costs, he is making an implicit assumption about which use should bear the costs, because **internalizing the costs to one use externalizes them to interfering uses**.

Now let us relax our assumption that the railroad and farmers cannot negotiate an enforceable agreement. Let us begin by asking what would happen if the railroad were held liable for the cost of fires. We already determined that without an agreement, the railroad would run 1 train. But, if it could "bribe" the farmers not to plant extra crops it could maximize its profits at $130 by running two trains. Thus, it will be willing to offer up to $100 to get the farmers not to plant the extra crops. The farmers, however, would be better off with any "bribe" in excess of $50, as that is their extra profit from planting additional crops. Assuming that the railroad and the farmers would evenly split the extra social wealth created by an agreement, the railroad would pay $75 to the farmers who would agree not to grow extra crops. The railroad will maximize profits by running two trains, earning a total of $55 ($130 in direct profit minus the $75 payment to the farmers). The farmers would not plant extra crops and would earn profits of $75, the payment they receive from the railroad. The resulting outcome would be efficient: the farmers would refrain from planting the extra crops and the railroad would run two trains.

Now suppose that the railroad had the legal entitlement; it did not have to pay for fires its trains started. Without an agreement we already determined that the railroad would run 3 trains and earn a $300 profit. But, under this scenario, farmers would bear $180 of the cost of fires. The farmers would save $60 in costs if they could pay the railroad not to run the third train. The railroad, however, only makes an extra $50 by running this train. Again assuming that the parties evenly split the social wealth created by their agreement, the farmers will pay a $55 "bribe" to get the railroad not to run the third train. The railroad will run 2 trains and earn $305 in profit ($250 in direct profit plus the $55 payment from the farmers). The farmers will not plant extra crops and will bear a cost of $175 ($120 in harm from fires and the $55 payment to the railroad). Again, the parties reach the efficient outcome—2 trains and no extra crops.

Having gone through the example, it is easy to see that Coase's Theorem holds in general. If a legal entitlement creates an incentive for a party to act inefficiently, there will be social wealth that can be gained by getting that party to agree not to act in the inefficient manner. It will therefore be in the interest of some other party, who bears the cost of the inefficient conduct by the first party, to bribe the first party not to act inefficiently. This also makes evident the second lesson of Coase's Theorem: **if transaction costs are zero, to maximize wealth society should pick the legal rule that is cheapest to administer, as every legal rule will lead to the wealth maximizing outcome.**

Coase's Theorem is significant because it changed the debate in law and economics much the way Adam Smith did for microeconomics. Just as Smith argued that social wealth is maximized by allowing free trade among individuals interested in pursuing their purely private wants, Coase argues that wealth is maximized by encouraging these same self-interested actors to trade legal entitlements. The analogy to Smith's competitive market is Coase's zero transaction cost society. Coase's Theorem thus alters the whole outlook of economic reasoning about law. Instead of trying to devise the legal rule that forces parties to behave in a wealth maximizing manner, the state should merely try to minimize transaction costs, thereby allowing private parties to reach the optimal outcome. Whereas traditional microeconomics counselled that government should tax those who impose external costs on society, Coase counsels that the government should create a property scheme in legal entitlements, allowing individuals to buy and sell them freely, without having to incur significant transaction costs to do so.

Several caveats about Coase's Theorem, however, are in order. First, even in a world of zero transaction costs, although every legal rule will lead to the efficient outcome, different legal rules will have different effects on the parties involved. In our example, making the railroads liable for fires that their trains start resulted in the farmers getting $75 in wealth and the railroad getting $55 in wealth. When we switched the entitlement so that the railroad was not liable (*i.e.*

the farmers bore the cost of fires started by the trains) the railroad ended up with $305 and the farmers with -$175. Thus the parties care greatly about the legal rule.[27] As a corollary, if we are concerned about fairness as well as wealth maximization, then Coase's Theorem does not necessarily provide the right approach to evaluation of legal rules.

Second, in the real world, transaction costs are never zero. Thus, parties frequently will not bargain to the efficient outcome. In practice, this means that legal decision-makers—legislators, judges, and the heads of administrative agencies—will have to choose between setting legal rules in a manner that minimizes transaction costs and thereby encourages private bargains, and regulating to require directly or encourage indirectly conduct that the decision-maker believes to be wealth maximizing. To evaluate such a choice, we must ask whether transaction costs can be made small enough that private parties have enough incentive to bargain to the efficient outcome. We must also consider whether the government will have the ability to accurately assess what conduct is efficient. Finally, we must compare the direct costs of administering the two approaches for getting to the efficient outcome: the cost of reaching, monitoring and enforcing private agreements versus the cost of formulating, monitoring and enforcing legal requirements.

Suggested Additional Reading

R.H. Coase, *The Problem of Social Cost*, 3 J. LAW & ECON. 1 (1960).

Robert C. Ellickson, *Of Coase and Cattle: Dispute Resolution Among Neighbors in Shasta County*, 38 STAN. L. REV. 627 (1986).

Donald H. Regan, *The Problem of Social Cost Revisited*, 15 J. LAW & ECON. 427 (1972).

Pierre Schlag, *An Appreciative Comment on Coase's* Problem of Social Cost: *A View from the Left*, 1986 WISC. L. REV. 919.

---

[27] Because changing the assignment of legal entitlements from one party to another results in a change in those parties' wealth, it is not necessarily the case that the legal rule will make no difference in the ultimate production and allocation of goods. Changing a legal entitlement may create a wealth effect that alters the wealth maximizing outcome. Therefore, Coase's Theorem can claim only that regardless of how a legal entitlement is assigned, the parties will bargain to an efficient outcome, although that outcome may not be the same efficient outcome as would result from a different assignment of the entitlement.

INDEX

adverse selection: described, 74-75
antitrust, 1
Arrow, Kenneth, 58,60
Arrow's Theorem, 58-59
average cost: defined, 24-25; relation to marginal cost, 25-27
Ayres, Ian, 90

Baird, Douglas G., 90
barriers to entry: in competitive markets in the long run, 37-38
Baumol, William J., 48
Beales, Howard, 68
Brealey, Richard, 84
Breyer, Stephen, 68
budget line: defined, 7; characteristics of, 7-8; algebraic formula for, 7, effect of price changes on, 11-12; mentioned 7-13 *passim*

certainty equivalent: defined, 72; and insurance, 74; and investments, 83
Coase, Ronald H., 91, 94
Coase's Theorem: and allocation of legal entitlements, 91; and transaction costs, 91; and efficient outcomes, 91, 93; and external cost, 91; and criteria for choosing legal rules, 93-94; and administrative cost, 93, 94; and distribution of wealth, 94
Coleman, Jules, 60
competitive market: defined, 35; marginal revenue for a firm in, 35-36; demand curve for a firm in, 36; and short run equilibrium, 36-37; and long run equilibrium, 37-38
consumers, 5-19 *passim*
consumer choice: and non-market transactions, 5, 50; reaction to price changes, 11-13; for borrowing and lending, 79-80
consumer preferences: theory of 5-10; exogeneity of, 10; for risk, 70-73
consumer sovereignty, 54
consumer surplus: defined, 16; relationship to the demand curve, 16-17; as a component of social wealth, 40
contract, 5; and strategic behavior, 85; reliance-breach game, 87, 89
contract law: and Price discrimination, 43-44
contract curve: in Edgeworth Box defined, 50; relation to Pareto optimality, 50-51
cost: *see* average cost, external cost, fixed cost, information cost, marginal cost, monitoring cost, opportunity cost, total cost, transaction cost, variable cost, cultural norms, 3

demand: relation to consumer choice, 5; individual functions, 13-14 demand curve: relation to individual demand function, 14; of a firm in a competitive market, 36; and equilibrium in a competitive market, 36-37; and changes in consumer taste, 44
Demsetz, Harold, 68

discounting of future value: 81
Dixit, Avinash K., 90
dominant strategy: defined, 86; for prisoner's dilemma, 86
Dworkin, Ronald, 60

economic model, example of, 2-3; potential inaccuracies of, 2-3; mentioned 1-2
economic rationality: mentioned, 1-2; of workers, 2-3 and n.2; psychology of, 3; and consumer choice, 5-6
Edgeworth Box: described, 49-51; and production, 52-53
efficiency: potential trade off with fairness, 3; mentioned 2-3; Pareto criteria for, 49; distributional, 49-51; productive, 51-52; allocative, 52-53; of investment in future production, 82
elasticity, *see* price elasticity
Ellickson, Robert C., 19, 94
Elster, Jon, 3
enforcement cost: described, 67
equilibrium: defined, 36 n.12; of competitive markets in the short run, 36-37; of competitive markets in the long run, 38; and changes in technology, 44, and changes in consumer taste, 44; and tax on production, 44-45; and price cap, 45-46; *see also* Nash Equilibrium
expected utility: defined, 71
expected value: defined, 69-70
external benefit: described, 65; and social value, 65; and level of production, 65-66; and public goods, 66
external cost: described, 63; and level of production, 64; and social cost, 64; internalization of, 64, 92; and Coase's Theorem, 92-93; reciprocity of 92
externality: described, 63

fairness: mentioned, 2; and price discrimination, 43; and Pareto optimality, 54; and wealth maximization, 55-56
Farber, Daniel A., 60
fixed cost: defined, 28
free rider problem, 66
Frickey, Philip P., 60
Friedman, Milton, 3, 19

game: defined, 85; strategy for, 85; normal form, 85-86; prisoner's dilemma, 85-86, 88; reliance-breach game, 87, 89; extensive form, 87-88
game theory, 85-90 *passim*; Nash Equilibrium, 86-87
Giffen good, 12 n.6

Hovenkamp, Herbert, 48
Hirsch, Werner Z., 3

imperfect information: defined, 66
income: as a constraint on consumer choice, 7
income effect: defined, 12-13; affect on allocation of legal rules, 94 n.27
income stream, 1; *see also* present value of an annuity
incomplete information: defined, 66
indifference curves: explained 6; characteristics of 6; stability of, 10; and Edgeworth Box, 50;
    for present versus future consumption, 79-80
inferior good, 12-13
information cost: described, 66; as a transaction cost, 67
information: incomplete, 66; imperfect, 66
insurance: and reduction of risk, 74, 76; and moral hazard, 74, 76-77; and adverse selection,
    74-75; example of, 75-77; effect of co-payments, 76-77
interest: explained, 779-80; relation to rate of return on investment, 82-83
interest group politics, 59-60; and cost of collective action, 59-60
investments in future production: described, 81-82; rate of return on, 82-83; and risk, 83-84;
    portfolio of 84; β of, 84
isocost lines: defined, 23; relation to point of least cost production, 23
isoquants: defined, 22; characteristics of, 22-23; relation to point of least cost production, 23

Johnson, Eric J., 73 n.20
justice, 2

Kahneman, Daniel, 73 n.20, 77
Kaldor-Hicks efficiency, 54-55
Klevorick, A.K., 3
Knight, Frank H., 3
Kronman, Anthony, 60

Leff, Arthur, 3
law of supply and demand, 36-37
leisure: economic value of, 22
log-rolling, 59
long run: defined, 28; competitive market in, 37
lost wages: value of, 1

macroeconomics, 1 n.1
Malkiel, Burton G., 84
Mansfield, Edwin, 19, 34, 48, 60, 68, 77, 84
marginal cost: defined, 24-25; relation to average cost, 25-27; and profit maximization, 29;
    example of, 32-33
marginal rate of product transformation: defined, 52; concavity of, 52; relation to allocative
    efficiency, 54
marginal rate of substitution: defined, 7; relationship to prices, 9; relation to distributional
    efficiency, 54; relation to allocative efficiency, 54

marginal rate of technical substitution, 54
marginal revenue: defined, 29; and profit maximization, 29; example of, 34; for a monopoly, 39-40
marginal utility: and rational choice, 5
market imperfections: 61-68 *passim*
Marris, Robin, 34
McAdams, Richard H., 19
microeconomics: defined, 1; descriptive aspects of, 2; normative aspects of, 2
minimum wage: efficiency of, 2
monitoring cost: described, 67
monopoly: mentioned, 1; defined, 39; marginal revenue curve for, 39-40; and restriction of output, 41; and economic profit, 41; and changing technology, 42; and price discrimination, 42-43; and contract law, 43-44; as a market imperfection, 61; *see also* natural monopoly
monopoly market, 39-44 *passim*
monopoly power: sources of, 61
monopoly rent, 41
moral hazard: defined, 74; example of, 76-77
Mueller, Dennis C., 34, 58 n.15
Myers, Stewart, 84

Nalebuff, Barry J., 90
Nash Equilibrium: defined, 86; significance of, 86-87
natural monopoly: criteria for 61-62; marginal cost curve for, 62; regulation of, 62-63; and development of technology, 64
negligence, 1
normal return: defined, 29
nuisance: and internalization of external cost, 64

oligopoly: and strategic behavior, 85
Olson, Mancur, 60
opportunity cost: defined, 21; contrasted with accounting cost, 21; example, 21-22

Pareto frontier: defined, 51
Pareto optimality: defined, 49; relation to contract curve, 50-51; and allocative efficiency, 53; and interpersonal utility comparisons, 54; bias towards the status quo, 54; and fairness, 54
Pareto superiority: defined, 49
patent: mentioned, 42; as legally sanctioned monopoly, 61
Pauly, Mark V., 77
Posner, Richard, A., 60
present value: mentioned, 1, 79; defined, 81; example calculation of, 81; of an annuity, 81; of a future life, 82-83; of a risky investment, 83-84
price cap: in a competitive market, 45; and social wealth, 45, 47; and illegal markets, 45; in a monopoly market, 47-48; and incentives to improve technology, 47

price elasticity: of demand, 14-15; relationship to the time frame, 15-16
price discrimination: described, 42-43; and distribution of social wealth, 42-43; and contract law, 43-44
prisoner's dilemma: normal form of, 85-86; extensive form of, 88
producers, 21-34 *passim*
production: decision to go into, 29, 34
production region: defined, 23
production possibilities curve: defined, 51-52
production inputs: described, 22; capital, 22-24; labor 22-24
probability distribution; of uncertain outcome defined, 70 n.18
profit: defined, 21, 28; and return on investment, 28; and normal return, 29; geometrical representation, 29-31; in competitive markets in the long run, 38; as a component of social wealth, 40; of a monopoly, 41
profit maximization: as the goal of producers, 21; relationship to marginal revenue and cost, 29; and quantity produced, 29; example of, 31-34
property rights: and Coase's Theorem, 93
public choice theory, 58
public goods: defined, 66; and level of production, 66

Rasmusen, Eric, 90
rate of return on investment: for a non-risky investment, 82; and risk, 83-84
rate regulation: of a natural monopoly, 62-63
rationality, *see* economic rationality
rational voting scheme, 58; for single peaked preferences, 59 n.16; and strategic voting, 59; and log-rolling, 59
Rawls, John, 56-57
Rawls' maximin principle: and social welfare, 56-57; and equality, 57
Regan, Donald H., 94
return on investment: relation to economic profit, 28; and risk, 83-84
risk: and uncertainty, 69; defined, 69; independence from expected value, 70; consumers' attitudes towards, 70, 71-73; cost of, 73; and insurance, 74; and rate of return on investment, 83-84; reduction by diversification, 84; systematic, 84
risk aversion: utility function for, 71; reasons for, 72-73; psychology of, 73 n.20
risk preference: utility function for, 71
risk premium, 72

Scherer, F.M., 48
Schlag, Pierre, 94
Schumpeter, Joseph A., 48
second best: theory of described, 67 n.17
short run: defined, 28; competitive market in, 36
Smith, Adam, 93
social wealth: defined, 40; relation to marginal cost and demand curves, 40-41

social welfare function: for wealth maximization, 55; for Rawls's maximin principle, 57; legislative determination of, 57-60
Stigler, George J., 34, 48
strategic behavior: and game theory, 85, 89
strategic voting, 59
strict liability, 1
subsidy: effect on consumer utility, 18-19; of public goods, 66
substitution effect: defined, 12-13
supply curve: in the short run, 36; affects of technology changes on, 44

tax: consumer response to, 5; and equilibrium in a competitive market, 45; and social wealth, 44-45; and internalization of an externality, 64, 93
Thaler, Richard, 19, 73 n.20
Thurow, Lester, 2 n.2
time value of money: reasons for, 79; relation to risk aversion, 79; and interest rate, 79-80
total cost: function mentioned 22, function derived, 23-24; relation to marginal cost, 24-25; relation to average cost, 26; example of, 32
transaction costs: as a market imperfection, 67; and Coase's Theorem, 91; legal rules in the absence of, 91; choice of legal rules in the presence of, 93; minimization of, 93-94
Tversky, Amos, 73 n.20, 77

utility: and consumer preferences, 6; interpersonal comparison of, 6, 54; maximization of 9; von Neumann-Morganstern function for, 70-72

variable cost: defined, 28; and the decision to remain in business, 30 n.7
variance: and risk, 70 n.19
Veljanovski, Cento, 3
Vickrey, William, 58 n.15

wealth: as a constraint on consumer choice, *see* income,
wealth effect, *see* income effect
wealth distribution: and social welfare, 49; impact on efficient outcomes, 54, 55-56
wealth maximization: defined, 55; and curves of equal social welfare 55; and valuation problems, 55; and bias towards the wealthy, 56; and fairness, 55-56; and equality, 56
welfare economics: defined, 49